Contents

Prologue

This publication documents the Movement Forum project and celebrates the relationships cultivated throughout the event. Theatrum Mundi (TM) organised and curated Movement Forum as a mobile laboratory in three European cities (London, Paris and Lisbon) to address urgent questions in the design of urban (im)mobilities. In that experimental journey we brought together spatial and choreographic practitioners as well as emerging creatives in the field of architecture to explore and develop methodologies in response to injustice and unsustainability in urban movement.

3 cities
3 workshops
6 days
4 emerging creatives
4 choreographic artists
30 days of intense movement
50 participants later

This edition follows our journey as an account of the embodied encounters that the experiment prompted. It arrives in your hands with the intention of serving as a printed archive as well as a resource of empirical thoughts that build on the methods and ideas proposed by previous Theatrum Mundi's publications on choreography, embodiment, and urban design. It resembles the format of a creative diary that records individual and collective actions, ideas, and feelings, and documents the retrospective reflections of the invited contributors and participants upon all those activities that occurred during two months and in three cities. The intention, more than anything else, is to offer radical and alternative approaches to urban design inspired by the disciplines of dance, movement, and performance to ensure more just and inclusive public life in cities.

Far from offering concrete solutions to specific questions and to known, felt but rarely addressed urban problems, the edition intends to remain incomplete, disordered, unassuming, and non-conclusive. It seeks to showcase new and experimental ways of thinking-of and making-with our bodies in the city. It hopes to raise awareness about our individual yet biased embodied experiences and the collective effort it takes to open up, understand, and embrace the experiences of others. It shares a vocabulary of words and gestures we developed together to help different professionals communicate better the needs and ambitions of design in buildings and cities. It also aspires to convey the continuity in the embodied understanding of space, as something that starts from within the body and merges into the wider urban environment. The documentation and reflections that follow in the next pages reveal our methodological approach to address with words and movement issues of mobility justice and implant seeds for new ideas, collaborations, and projects in the future.

The book is structured chronologically following the sequence of the labs, from London to Paris and finally Lisbon, and each chapter includes contributions from the curators, workshop leaders, and participants. Three more contributions from the à la sauvette collective (a 2021 Future Architecture fellow) and Rebecca Faulkner (Theatrum Mundi's former research placement on the *Embodying Otherness* edition) propose alternative narratives that span all three labs, connect the dots between people and places, and weave the intellectual threads and embodied experiences together. In the end, *Encounters* is a collection of ideas, stories, and voices of the architects, dancers, urbanists, and choreographers who contributed to our experiment, discussing the process they went through, the conversations they held, but mainly the encounters they had along the way. Encounters that challenged not only the way they relate to each other but also the way they are, move, and co-exist in urban and natural spaces; the way they present themselves, embody their identities and accommodate the identities and presence of others; and the way they relate to other non-human species and inanimate things with whom they share their habitat. It is exactly these encounters, whether amorous, meaningful, lasting, intimate, conscious or not, that this publication ultimately wants to narrate and celebrate.

Each of the contributions is an experiment in format and perspective of writing. Each focuses on a type of encounter the author had, with others, with a place, with themselves, with architecture, with the city, with nature, or with time, and discusses or reflects upon any of the aspects of those encounters, whether that is the idea, the experience or the people, the senses, the textures, the language, the interactions, the methodologies, the sounds, or the memories involved. The encounters and their discussions are linked to the themes of the different labs and the initial questions of the Movement Forum project about spatial and choreographic thinking in the design of urban mobilities.

We would like to thank all the people who contributed to this edition for their brilliant and thoughtful ideas, their generosity in sharing, and their firm belief and invested passion in the scope of the work. We are also grateful to our contributing designers and illustrators, Marcos Villalba, Santiago Confalonieri, and Marcello Licitra, who helped visually strengthen the content of this edition, as well as to the Future Architecture Platform and Creative Europe who have financially supported the Movement Forum project and resulting edition.

We hope that you enjoy reading about our encounters and we encourage you to find and create your own with the help of our words and gestures. Go search for other bodies in other places, in space, in time. This is our invitation for an encounter and an act of love.

Fani Kostourou

Movement Forum
[Fani Kostourou and Elahe Karimnia]

Movement Forum focused on the design of urban (im)mobilities across European cities and asked the question: How can new forms of interdisciplinarity between city-making and dance-making help engender care for bodies, both human and non-human, in urban landscapes? The project responded to the increasing need for more socially and environmentally sustainable ways to think about city-making based on care in interactions of materials and flows, human and non-human bodies. Owing an intellectual debt to the concept of 'mobility justice' introduced by Mimi Sheller in 2018, its aim was to share existing positions and practices, while mapping mobility injustices in different settings.

Theatrum Mundi, as the latest institutional member of the Future Architecture (FA) platform, was invited to propose and implement a programme of architectural events in Europe that would explore new models of creative and collaborative work, involving creatives of different generations and disciplines who applied to the FA's annual Call for Ideas. Within the framework of the Movement Forum, the selected fellows had the opportunity to develop, present, and test their submitted ideas through multidisciplinary exchanges and encounters with artists and practitioners from Theatrum Mundi's own network.

Journey

In Autumn 2021, we organised three workshops in three European cities, London, Paris and Lisbon, in collaboration with artists, architects, and choreographic practitioners as well as institutional partners from different cities. The labs encouraged new forms of collaboration to explore how new and shared methodologies spanning their reciprocal fields can be developed in response to an embodied understanding of injustice and unsustainability in urban movement.

Theatrum Mundi first approached à la sauvette collective to develop their Dance is Politics idea, using the 'party' and dancing as a methodology to explore the appropriation of public space in each city. The team was asked to stage one 'party' in each city, designing interventions *in situ* and in collaboration with a local choreographer invited by Theatrum Mundi. We then reached out to three more emerging creatives, fem_arc, Soft Agency and Dancing Architects, to develop and lead activities in London, Paris and Lisbon respectively, based on their submitted ideas to the FA Call for Ideas. Over the summer of 2021 and through several online meetings, we managed to connect the various contributors and artists, build a common theoretical foundation, and collaborate to translate ideas into bodily experiments.

Actions

The workshops focused on different themes pertinent to the context of each city:

The London Lab (18–19 Sept 2021) focused on the themes of Power and Gender. à la sauvette (Las Palmas de Gran Canaria) and fem_arc collectives (Berlin) exchanged ideas and practices with the choreographer and researcher Sara Wookey, who partnered with engineer, interdisciplinary researcher, and dancer Ellie Cosgrove. Altogether they gave prompts, led walks, and staged parties to investigate the temporary transformation of public space via self-managed celebrations. The London-based activities took place around the Clerkenwell area, inside the Smithfield Market and in the public realm of the Barbican Estate. Sara Wookey led a choreographic walk in different public and private spaces across the city, while Lara Stöhlmacher and Noumissa Sidibé from fem_arc collective ran F_WALKS, an audiowalk on emancipatory spatial practices, which exposed participants to stories about the feminist appropriation of urban spaces and the ways they facilitate the reassessment of female bodies in the city. The discussion took place in Theatrum Mundi's office in 15A Clerkenwell Close, a building designed by Amin Taha and Groupwork, which was shortlisted for the RIBA Stirling Prize in 2021.

The Paris Lab (1-2 Oct 2021) adopted another take on Movement Forum's questions, looking at Wildness and Queer Counter-Publics in the city. Over two days, the performer and activist Habibitch (Algiers, Paris), Soft Agency (Berlin) and à la sauvette collectives explored choreographic and embodied approaches in relation to city-making processes by both humans and non-humans through storytelling, voguing, walking, and reading. Habibitch gave a waacking workshop and performance lecture on Decolonising the Dancefloor about the history of violence inflicted on queer and colonised bodies and how the ballroom has been a form of resistance against oppression. Rosario Talevi from Soft Agency guided a Parasitic Reading Room, which took the form of an open, spontaneous, and travelling session through *Parc des Beaumonts*, inviting participants to read aloud a selection of texts on wilderness and rewilding. The workshop was held at Opale, a meanwhile space for creativity and solidarity managed by Plateau Urbain in Montreuil. The party was initially planned to take place in the woods of *Bois de Vincennes*; however, due to weather conditions it was moved inside and later transferred to *Ateliers Médicis* in *Clichy-sous-Bois* with a smaller group of participants.

The Lisbon Lab (16-17 Oct 2021) dealt with the Topographies of Body and Landscape. For this workshop, Theatrum Mundi partnered with Lisbon Architecture Triennale, another FA institutional member, as well as the choreographer, dancer, and artistic director of BODYBUILDERS, Rafael Alvarez (Lisbon), the architectural theorist Takako Hasegawa from Dancing Architects (Tokyo, London), and à la sauvette collective.[1] Rafael Alvarez hosted a contemporary dance workshop, Something, that proposed to explore and develop a collection of bodyscapes based on the personal movement vocabulary of each participant. The activity ended with a site-specific performative party, Something in Between, aiming to choreograph invisible lines that connect us and simultaneously drive us apart. The next day, Takako Hasegawa hosted a choreographic workshop, Textures of gestures/Movement glossary, exploring the translation of physical touches, spatial memories and felt senses into movement vocabularies. The participants experienced the varying relationships between movement, space, and body, especially in relation to the topography of the Portuguese capital. Most activities took place in the courtyard and interiors of Palácio Sinel de Cordes, eventually surging into the city and the immediate urban surroundings of Campo de Santa Clara. Although Pablo Castillo, Ernesto Ibáñez and Héctor Suárez from à la sauvette collective were physically absent

---

1   The members of à la sauvette collective did not physically join the Lisbon Lab due to their participation in the programme of another FA member. However, their intervention was set up by the Theatrum Mundi team.

from the lab, their third and final intervention of their Three parties in Wonderland project, created a spatial narrative that bridged the gap between the three cities and culminated in asking: how public is public space?

Cast

Movement Forum was curated and organised by Theatrum Mundi staff members, Fani Kostourou (TM Associate Director), Elahe Karimnia (former TM Associate, now TM Advisor) and John Bingham-Hall (TM co-Director) with the support of Lou Marcellin (TM Outreach Manager) on communications and PR. The documentation of all three labs was done by Rebecca Faulkner, TM's former research placement, who was responsible for mapping and reflecting on the bodily experiences and design strategies that emerged as a result of the various activities. Finally, the Lisbon Lab was filmed by Vítor Hugo Costa, who produced a short film that documented the experiments of the Lisbon Lab and helped reach a wider audience.

Of course, the project as well as this edition are collective efforts and processes. It goes without saying that Movement Forum would not have been able to happen – nor culminate in what we hope was a memorable, joyful, and sensual learning journey – without the support of the Future Architecture Platform, Groupwork, Plateau Urbain, and Lisbon Architecture Triennale; the brilliant contributions of the aforementioned emerging creatives, artists, choreographers, dancers, architects, researchers, and colleagues; as well as a number of genuinely enthusiastic participants from across Europe: Adam Moore, Amandine Canistro, Andrés Avila Reyes, Anna Sofia Lekander, Anna Ulrikke Andersen, Aseem Inam, Bárbara Araque Palacios, Christian Kipp, Diego Jenowein, Dimitri Szuter, Ellie Cosgrove, Eloise Maltby Maland, Ernesto Ibáñez Galindo, Eunsoo Jang, Gloria Calderone, Habibitch, Helene,

Héctor Suárez González, Iro Xyda, Joanna Kuczora, Joseph Kai, Julia Albani, Lara Stöhlmacher, Laura Davy, Laura Narvaez Zertuche, Lee Campbell, Luc Sanciaume, Mahsa Alami, Marta Michalowska, Marzia Magnanini, Mikaela Psarra, Noumissa Sidibé, Oceane Ragoucy, Pablo Castillo Luna, Phoebe Eddleston, Rafael Alvarez, Rebecca Faulkner, Rosario Talevi, Rui Filipe Antunes, Sara el Samman, Sara Wookey, Sebastien Millot, Stephanie, Takako Hasegawa, Victoria Noakes, and Youmna Saba. For all that and more, we thank you warmly. Not only are we very grateful to you for your efforts, passion, and patience, but also to all those who helped us make it possible whilst creating and sharing an enjoyable experience for the mind, body, and soul.

Looking ahead

The next stop in this journey is Three parties in Wonderland, a public event that will take place in October 2022 within the framework of the Lisbon Architecture Triennale 2022 and will build on the experiments that took place during the Movement Forum. In a scenography inspired by the dancefloor and installed in the garden of the Museu Nacional de Arte Contemporânea in Lisbon, Theatrum Mundi and à la sauvette collective will offer a day of performative interventions that will open the eyes and bodies in three acts. In each act, an artist will invite the public to follow a choreographed action, designed to explore a specific issue of movement in the city. The acts will be able to be experienced individually or in a sequence as part of an immersive day in which we will gradually dive into Wonderland to transform our bodies and identities.

We invite you to experience this mystical transformation through the pages of this book.

How Alice
Found the Path

Among all the books you can find on my shelf, there is one with a special story behind it. It starts when during one of my many trips through Central and Northern England, I entered an old bookstore with an austere but welcoming appearance. Once inside, I found this one book with no title or illustration on its worn cover, which rapidly caught my attention. As I began to skim through its pages, my curiosity spiked, so I ran to the bookseller to inquire about this little gem of a book. The eager man, somewhat eccentric but certainly talkative, told me it was a tale published before *Alice in Wonderland*, the famous novel written by Lewis Carroll. I had once heard something about it, but I had only thought it was gossip, a tittle-tattle from the elderly academics. Very few people had read it, and there were even fewer copies preserved. The lucky bookseller had come across this copy in a stall of a small flea market near there. Now to let you understand the importance of the discovery, I would like to reproduce below an excerpt of that book that I found of great interest.

‡

Alice woke up with some make-up still on. Like every other morning, she looked out the window just in front of her bed. Even though she was wishing for a sunny morning, that day had started grey as if everyone had agreed to be in a bad mood at the same time, and that horrible headache wasn't helping either.

The night before hadn't been particularly fun, but that didn't stop her from arriving home just as dawn was breaking. She hadn't been enjoying the nights out with her friends that much lately. Same old faces, same old music, same old superior looks of people she was starting to get tired of.

When she finally went out that morning to do her chores, the only thing she really wanted was to run back home. The noise, the traffic, people in a hurry... just like being in a party, feeling like a piece that didn't quite fit into a mechanism that wouldn't stop working.

While she was walking down the street, she saw something glowing incredibly bright in the distance. It was a different light, not like a street lamp or a road sign. And yet somewhat inexplicably, it seemed ordinary, like a strange but familiar glow that she thought she had seen a million times before. Even from afar, she could smell the scuffed soles, the alcohol, the dancefloor sweat, and the smoke. She could also hear some music, although inconspicuous. The closer she reached the end of the street, the stronger the glow seemed to grow.

The brightness led her to what appeared to be a huge mirror. Standing in front of it, Alice could see her faithful reflection, herself being on the same drab inglorious and noisy street she was. But looking through the opposite side of the mirror, the atmosphere was very different: hundreds of people partying and dancing in the middle of a street that looked identical to the one behind her, sided by the same cars, facing the same houses. No more long faces, no people rushing past. Just good vibes, enchanting music, and smiles.

Alice wished with all her might to be part of that joyful celebration. 'It seems much more fun than this boring city and my boring chores!' And before she could notice it, as if by magic, she leaped through to the other side, swaying rhythmically to the beats of the music amidst a dense and jovial crowd. She was feeling wonderful, as if nothing could go wrong anymore, hardly recalling how bleak her day had been until that very moment. Witnessing so many people having a good time in the same street she walked before suddenly made the city look less dull, even if its image hadn't changed a bit.

That strange but familiar glow that had led Alice through the mirror before, suddenly began to move. Alice was the only one to notice at first. Captivated by its eeriness, she tagged along. Her crisscrossing pursuit urged the rest of the crowd who decided to follow her. With the music still on, the cheerful and excited mass dance-walked down the street, turned around a few corners, passed arrays of buildings and trees, and, before realising it, ended up in the middle of a dense forest. And yet, no one seemed willing to stop the party.

The forest looked a little bit cold and dark. Still, with all these people around, Alice did not feel unsafe. The glow made her look down her feet, in front of which a pink path had made its way, transforming into a catwalk. She could see it disappearing over the horizon, winding through the trees, as if someone had just painted it over to show the way. Okay, this is the strangest day of my life, that's for sure, she thought, as she realised that the partying crowd danced along the pink path.

The deeper they advanced into the woods, the more the catwalk began to resemble a parade. No one from the crowd knew where the pink path was leading, but they were all enjoying the journey, laughing and celebrating together. Alice met lots of people along the way, from the farthest corners of the world, each carrying the most incredible story. Wow, it has been a while since I had such a good time!, she thought.

Due to her short stature, soon came a point where Alice could only see heads, shoulders, necks, and a few elbows. Poor Alice, the pink path was the only thing that kept her going. She realised she had to break free from the crowd. Struggling to make room between moving bodies, Alice soon sneaked into the courtyard of a beautiful palace. Nothing seemed more oddly positioned near the edge of the forest.

Above the palace, the stars and the moon shone brightly. For some time now, she couldn't locate the strange familiar glow. But she knew she no longer needed it. At that moment, Alice felt good. It had been a really long time since she last felt this way. And in her blissfulness, she could tell the sounds were louder, the colours brighter, and the smells more intense. On this side of the mirror, she could feel her body more present than ever.

Although the party continued, it was for her time to leave. She scrambled out of the crowd and started her way out. Such a fantastic night, her thoughts silently roaring. The dawn was breaking splendidly. Alice had only moved a few metres away from the palace when suddenly a White Rabbit with pink eyes ran close by her. There was nothing so very remarkable in that; nor did Alice think it so very much out of the way to hear the Rabbit say to itself, Oh dear! Oh dear! I shall be too late!

‡

Ever since I first read this story in that bookshop, I have not been able to get it out of my head. The story ends where Alice in Wonderland begins, as a way for readers to delve into Alice's mystical world and understand the motivations behind her numerous adventures. The book is really about those little things that transform potentially monotonous and dull everyday rituals into welcoming and exciting life-changing experiences. And by little things, I mean the party and how it was a transformative tool for Alice's perception of the streets, the city, and the people living in them.

Anyway, this is what I think, but who knows, I may also be reading too much into this old book. It doesn't matter, because I am sure the music, the dance, the beats, the colours and lights, the crowd, the parade, the catwalk and the dancefloor that Alice experienced on that mirroring side, really changed her life. In fact, I am convinced they did.

‡

Three parties in Wonderland
[à la sauvette]

The tale 'How Alice found the path' narrated how a party has the potential to transform the urban environment. This is far from being fiction. In fact, self-managed celebrations such as block parties or raves have proved to be an essential tool for reclaiming urban spaces and the freedom of movement for marginalised and underrepresented collectives.

In the framework of the Movement Forum, which addressed questions of mobility justice in relation to design, we approached the party's transformative capacity from the perspective of its design. To explore that, we staged three parties across three cities, in London, Paris and Lisbon. Our project, Three Parties in Wonderland, aimed to performatively test the relationship between movement and design, using the *party* as a programmatic experiment that can temporarily transform the socio-spatial conditions of cities and reveal injustices in the use and access of public space. Through the staging of self-managed celebrations in different settings, the project empirically explored how these celebrations entail an opportunity to challenge established power dynamics that shape human and non-human mobilities in the cities.

Each party started with the design of a site-specific intervention tailored to its urban context. Each intervention staged a different theme: Power and Gender in London, Wildness and Queer Counter-Publics in Paris, and Topographies of Body and Landscape in Lisbon. Inspired by the universe of *Alice in Wonderland*,[1] we put forward a narrative that linked the three

themes and laboratories as three separate chapters of a single story. The story sought to invite the public to experiment and interact with the physical interventions in a fictional manner, reflecting upon the publicness of urban space.

The project kicked off with the intervention Through The Looking-Glass in London, which aimed to explore concepts of intimacy and exposure at the threshold between the private and public space. Once the looking-glass was crossed, the narrative continued in Paris with The Woods Where Things Have No Name, which looked at liminal spaces and the entanglements between humans and non-humans. The story ended in Lisbon with the chapter The Right Size?, which interrogated the relationship between the scale of the body and that of the environment.

Through The Looking-Glass

When one goes out, does one want to be seen or not? Does one want to shine on the dancefloor or indulge themselves in the music and go unnoticed? This idea, explored by the writer and editor Andrew Pasquier[2] elaborates on the mysticism surrounding the act of nightclubbing. When thinking about the experiential component of a night out, memories and experiences occupy a space between fiction and reality. The party is an alternative sphere that is not governed by the same rules of everyday life. It embraces

1   Carroll, L. (1865) *Alice's Adventures in Wonderland.*

2   Pasquier, A. (2020) "Nightlife Architecture: From Times Square To The Spectrum, What We Get Out Of Going Out", *PIN–UP* 27, Fall Winter 2019/20 [archive.pinupmagazine.org/articles/essay-nightlife-architecture-paradise-basement-spectrum-andrew-pasquier]

different behaviours than those socially accepted in society. Is it only the mood, or is it also the spatial characteristics of such places that induce a change in the behaviour? If the physical environment can affect feelings of intimacy or exposure, how can the design of the cities cater for that?

Sociologist, Mimi Sheller, argues that marginalised groups find their access to public space limited due to surveillance mechanisms – 'for example through policies that prevent homeless people and "vagabonds" from sitting or lying down, that force "sex workers" into delimited zones for "street-walking," that push sidewalk-vendors out of prime locations, or that empower police to "stop and frisk" people of color.'[3] In essence, some social or political movements, identities, and collectives need to stay away from the spotlight so that they can exist. Different degrees of visibility and accessibility in public space were made explicit with the design intervention, Through The Looking-Glass. The idea behind it was to reinvent the threshold between two parallel realities: the public and the private, the visible and the invisible.

The intervention consisted of a silver curtain, hung from the façade of 15A Clerkenwell Close at the entrance of its side pathway – a quintessential semi-public space in London – and intangible elements such as lights, smoke, and music. The shiny curtain delineated the threshold between public and private but, like in *Alice in Wonderland*, acted as a mirror that lured people on both realms to cross to the other side. This minimal intervention invited people to interact with the curtain and experience how it affects their behaviour differently on either side of the 'mirror'. The public side of the threshold was believed to be more accessible and inclusive than the

building's pebbled pathway, yet it was more exposed to the public eye, and thus more restrictive in the kinds of social behaviours it would allow. Because public space is as public as the rules and power structures which govern that space allow it to be, the party thrown behind the curtain acted as a programmatic mechanism to temporarily abolish these rules and power structures.

The Woods Where Things Have No Name

The second intervention, The Woods Where Things Have No Name, took place in the *Bois de Vincennes*, in the outskirts of Paris. This vast public park has witnessed multiple intertwined stories that exemplify the multifaceted nature of human and non-human relations. The same forest has been a place for family gatherings and a space for cruising; a royal hunting preserve and a haven for wildlife; a place where African immigrants were forced into prostitution and a picnic area; a zoological park as well as a colonial botanical garden. Different forms and histories of human and non-human (im) mobilities have been entangled in this space, from the exertion of control and power abuse to the self-management of behaviour outside what is socially accepted. The degree of publicness of this park differs from the cloister-like space where London Lab was hosted. Situated between the opaque and the hidden, this place not only belongs to the everyday life of the Parisians – being close to the city and accessible from it – but also operates at its margins.

Conceptually, the *Bois de Vincennes* fits into what the philosopher Michel Foucault called *heterotopias*,[4] a world within a world that is somehow 'other' and works parallel to society, while supporting its 'frictionless' function. Hospitals,

3   Sheller, M. (2018) *Mobility Justice: The Politics of Movement in an Age of Extremes,* pp. 111-12.

4   Foucault, M. (1967) "Of Other Spaces". *Diacritics*, 16 (1): 22-27.

cemeteries, and prisons are examples of this concept. These places embrace populations who become marginalised by a normative understanding of society. Likewise, the park and the party can be framed with a similar idea, the concept of *liminality*. As the cultural anthropologist Victor Turner describes it, liminality is 'a collective and creative transformation of identity, time, and space, separated from everyday reality'.[5] The liminal condition of the Parisian park has over the years allowed it to embrace alternative practices, species, and identities. Operating at the spatial and social margins of the city, it offers multiplicity instead of exclusion, challenging the normative rules that govern the rest of the city's public spaces.

In *Alice in Wonderland*, Alice and the fawn forget their names when they enter Tulgey wood. They walk together across it, embracing each other without remembering the categories that once divided them. When they finally reach the end of the woods, the fawn recalls his animal condition, and scared, it runs away from Alice.

The Woods Where Things Have No Name, the second intervention of the Three Parties in Wonderland project, continued the exploration of the publicness of public space from the sidelines. Following on from the first chapter of the story, the 'looking-glass' – the silver curtain of the London Lab – was present in this second staging, as if the woods were on the other side of the mirror.

In front of the curtain was now a bright pink path – another element inspired by Lewis Caroll's book. In *Alice in Wonderland*, the pink trail did not follow any signs; still, it directed Alice's movement in a way that was foreign to her and the environment. In contrast, the pink path in the *Bois de Vincennes* was designed as a catwalk for waacking. Waacking is a dance movement that originated in the 1970s gay clubs of Los Angeles, where 'poor Black, Latino, and Asian men found the freedom to express themselves through movement, despite the oppressive environments they faced in day-to-day life'.[6] The appropriation of the pink path and the subversion of its fictional use for dancing purposes added a new layer to the project narrative, that of staging movement to establish presence and fight oppression.

The Right Size?

The third intervention, The Right Size?, took place in the Palácio Sinel de Cordes, in Lisbon, and explored the theme Topographies of Body and Landscape. The topography of the city, like that of the palace itself, is irregular; its configuration and materials only embrace certain kinds of mobilities. The courtyard of the Palácio features two types of stairs. The first staircase, symmetric and grand, constitutes a symbol of power and gives access to the patio. On the contrary, small outdoor steps spread along the courtyard and although they may go unnoticed to certain bodies, they end up limiting the mobility of others. The two types of stairs are frequently found in the Portuguese city and their design, in combination with that of other architectural elements, hinders the physical access and publicness of many of its public spaces.

Issues in the scale of the design are also addressed in Lewis Carroll's book. Alice's body is constantly scaling up and down throughout the book. She is always finding herself too small or too big for her surroundings, but never the 'correct'

5   Turner, V. (1982) *From Ritual to Theatre: The Human Seriousness of Play.*

6   Ma, J. (2021), "What is Whacking (Waacking)?", *STEEZY* Blog [steezy.co/posts/waacking-voguing]

size.[7] Acknowledging that individual bodies differ significantly, how could anyone blame Alice for not being the right size for her environment?

The last intervention of Three Parties in Wonderland, The Right Size? aimed to reveal how differences in the topography and scales of the city affect the mobility of human bodies and stress the consequent inequalities of their design. The pink path that began in the *Bois de Vincennes,* wound its way from the tree to the symmetric stairs and through the courtyard, 'erasing' its stepped topography. It led straight to a banner asking: *How public is public space?* On the one hand, the question implied it is the city, and not the bodies, that coerce mobilities. Mobility is not limited per se, but always in relation to something else. On the other hand, the banner summarised the ideas from all three labs and cities, addressing the right to access public space: physically, legally, and psychologically.

The Right Size? explored a third degree of publicness of space. Inside the Palácio, there are several level changes and staircases before one can reach the courtyard from the street, and visits are often subject to public events. However, the limited accessibility of the space is not only a matter of land ownership and opening hours, but also the result of a design that does not accommodate non-able bodies and cannot adapt to different mobilities. Space is as inclusive as its design allows it to be and the degree of its publicness depends on the power the design exerts over bodily movements. Then it is worth asking: what kind of power do we have over public space? Do we have agency in defining its publicness? Do we assume its public condition, or can we transform it and make it our own?

Operating in the city can be approached from many different perspectives. Although architects often resort to reshaping the physical aspects of the built environment, there is a need to approach urban design as sociologists, proposing things that are more immaterial and intangible than physical. By introducing the party as a key design tool for the temporary transformation of spaces in all three cities, we aimed to adopt a social approach to design, putting collectivity at the centre of change. If we need to change the city, is there a better way to do it than partying?

---

7   Kostourou, F. and Psathiti, C. (2018) "What's wrong with Wonderland?". *trans magazin* 32, pp.78-82.

Undisciplined
[Rebecca Faulkner]

Across London, Paris, and Lisbon, my role was a peculiar one. Straddling observer, documenter, and participant all at once. Being simultaneously aware of and present in my own body, whilst actively observing my fellow attendees' collective and individual bodies. At times I felt like a surveillance object, an all-seeing eye static within a sea of motion. It felt strangely powerful. What would resonate with me? What would I choose to capture with the camera, note down or diagram?

In what follows, I offer my own account of the essence of the Movement Forum, which includes a selection of revelatory moments in a non-chronological order as well as emerging themes, conversations, and personal questions I asked myself during the experiment. Questions such as how can we, through collective enactments, create a shared awareness of the city, self, others, and their relational capacity? How can we *contaminate* public space and leave residual traces of shared experiences? How could these, in turn, begin to create an embodied vocabulary beyond the realms of language? In London, the first of the labs, collective enactments were a mechanism to create a collective awareness. On the second day, fem_arc's Audiowalk On Emancipatory Spatial Practices steered us quietly through a series of scenarios narrated by field recordings, sounds from other cities, and testimonies describing discrimination, exclusion, and resistance in public space. Documenting the walk, what would have been a solitary physical experience for listening, was a strangely intimate experience with Eloise, one of the participants and my chosen photographic subject. I think I attached myself to her because of a sense of familiarity, a feeling that we may have had similar city experiences and an expectation she may carry me down a path I would have tread on my own. One hundred metres behind, amongst a crowd of people going about their daily life, I was bound by Eloise's route choice, her pace, and her chosen moments of stillness in bold defiance of the rhythmic norms of the city. Paradoxically, she was being followed, watched, scrutinised, and ultimately bound to my voyeuristic activity, caught in a dialogue between observer and observed. A particularly poignant moment occurred when legs and arms splayed, head tilted to the sky, she lingered, whilst the audio walk was pushing us to be motionless for just longer than one may usually feel comfortable. On the flip side, her later decision to traverse a playground was uncomfortable. As a childless person, I sensed I needed an excuse or reason to be there. Wielding a camera, I was aware I could be perceived as threatening. This sense of needing to have a purpose in public spaces was echoed in other participants' experiences of daily city life. How often do we rely on phones, objects, and deliberate acts of walking, commuting, or waiting around to grant us legitimacy and signal visual cues to fellow city-goers that we have permission to be there?

Permission

Permission, what enables or disables us to access the city and what can disrupt that, was a continual theme throughout the Movement Forum. In Lisbon, the stepped nature and irregular terrain of our host site, the Palácio Sinel de Cordes, mirrored the topographical reality of the Portuguese capital. A limiting urban environment to

people with prams, people with accessibility or other mobility issues and anyone who may struggle to ascend the City of Lights. Scaling the streets, stairs, and infrastructures to the Palace each day was a stark reminder of how much Lisbon, and many other cities, cater for certain body types and body topographies. The narrow, uneven pavements, and slick textures of the city further contribute to this hostile environment. The lack of consideration or imagination of how other bodies may navigate and access the city was evident. To better design for more diverse bodies, we need social, spatial, and material justice.

In the third Lisbon Lab, my role most notably shifted from that of an observer to that of a participant. The presence of other documenters liberated me from my duties on the fringes, enabling me to 'record' the lab through my own body – quite literally – pressing myself into the dirt, folding into railings, melding with stairs, feeling with and through my body. As a group, moving into Campo de Santa Clara (the adjacent public realm and our stage), we enacted our newfound gestural vocabulary in a shared setting. I felt that props that resembled those studied in the palace courtyard were reassuring dance partners in rendering familiar objects and newly strange and wondrous environments.[1] Fences, railings, and bollards – all arguably hostile in that they often deny entrance and create urban (im)mobilities – were hacked, reappropriated, and reimagined as friendly, playful, soft, pliable, and supportive entities.

Anonymity

While our matching black outfits afforded me a sense of anonymity as an actor, encountering this very public and

traditionally non-theatrical space affected my presence. With the camera rolling and the audience watching, gestures that felt like research inside the Palácio Sinel de Cordes became performed. Perversely, our informal audience had no choice in their role as spectators. In blurring the line between research and performance, momentarily, we 'contaminated'[2] their public realm. Our staged, filmed, and anonymous performance provided us with the necessary legitimacy to infest space unapologetically, capturing fleeting imitations of a better world.[3]

Across the labs, I had a sense of safety in my anonymity, shifting between a 'fly on the wall' to one of the many bodies in a crowd. Anonymity, however, is a *privilege*; it is a choice not everyone has or can make if they want to. The privilege highlights the tension between unapologetically infesting public space and suffering no repercussions, when so many bodies are policed and restricted. The swarming nature in which we descended into the public realm drew attention. Whilst it disrupted the social codes and norms of being in public, I wonder if it also disrupted other people's access to public space and ability to be present.

Bodies talk

In Paris, workshop leader Habibitch spoke of their own experience and history of Algerian exclusion from the French narrative. In many ways, the denial of one's existence and anonymity are not too dissimilar. The difference lies in who is calling the shots.

1 Hendren, S (2020), *What Can a Body Do? How We Meet the Built World*.

2 Soft Agency introduced the term in the Parasitic Reading Room, led in Paris. The parasitic element denoted *infesting* the public realm, reading aloud together, and taking up space without asking for permission, whilst we, as readers, felt our way through the texts, shifting between chorus and monologue, and amplifying a multitude of voices. It was loud and unapologetic.

3 Dolan, J. (2005) *Utopia in Performance: Finding hope at theatre*, p. 2.

Too often, sociology creates *categories*, telling people who they are and denying them the ability to self identify. The historical French Colonial rule, which imposed ambiguous identities[4] on the Algerian communities, underpins the promotion of 'Frenchness' to this day, forcing people to shed their cultural heritage.[5] 'But where there is oppression, there is resistance'.[6] Whilst sharing and teaching us how to waack,[7] Habibitch presented how the ballroom scene has been a place of such resistance for them and many more. The gestural language of voguing and waacking are used when other means are taken away from those who wish to speak. In their energetic, almost euphoric, workshop, Habibitch shared with us how dance can be a resilient practice, a way to express everything from struggles and oppression to freedom and joy.[8] Dance is democratic, it can be done alone, it can be done together, it can be done anywhere and anytime.

Language

Dance (or movement), like architecture, is a visual art. Across the three labs, bodily gestures served as a common universal language for all the participants. In Lisbon, the verbal prompts given by the

workshop leaders, Rafael Alvarez and Takako Hasegawa, coupled with our own reactions to the built form of the Palace and the stage set crafted by à la sauvette collective, created internal, personal scores. Over two days, we moved and repeated these movements until they became a language, a lexicon of gestures. The process was not dissimilar to how we construct ourselves in reality. Our identity is always defined in relation to others and our actions shift, reacting to encounters with the built environment. Interactions and feelings of personal safety are forever in flux, foregrounded by the time of day, the season, the weather, and we configure our bodies to signal this to other city dwellers. Not only do our bodies keep the score of moments of fear, harassment, violence, and unwanted contact in public and private spaces,[9] but cultural references are also embedded into our movement choices. Our posture, facial expressions, gestures, eye contact, stance, muscle tension, walking style are moulded by navigating the urban environment,[10] the sediments and residue of which – whether negative or positive – continue to seep into everyday life, further reinforcing and solidifying the way we choose to communicate and express ourselves.

Perhaps rather than asking 'how public is public space',[11] we should consider how public are performing bodies?

Undisciplined

As I experienced through the Movement Forum, choreographers and movement specialists have other ways of analysing space. Comparatively, the tools and training

4   Bechiche, H. (2020), "Unveiling France's hidden histories in Algeria holds the key to understanding its modern Islamophobia", *gal-dem* [gal-dem.com/france-islamophobia/]

5   Ibid.

6   Habibitch (2021), *Decolonising the Dancefloor*, lecture notes, delivered 1 October 2021.

7   Whacking (originally punking) is a dance style that emerged from empowerment and strength in the LA gay community reclaiming the derogatory term punk as a positive action verb.

8   Habibitch (2021), "Habibitch: Algerian Non-Binary Boss Femme Aiming To Decolonize The Dancefloor", *MyKali Magazine* 73 [mykalimag.com/en/2021/09/18/habibitch-algerian-non-binary-boss-femme-aiming-to-decolonize-the-dance-floor/]

9   Bessel, A. van der Kolk (2014) *The Body Keeps the Score: Brain, Mind, and Body in the Healing of Trauma.*

10 Kern, L. (2019) *The Feminist City.*

11 à la sauvette (2021), *Dance is Politics*, lecture notes, delivered 18 September 2021.

of the architect are somehow restrictive; we receive abstract general knowledge and go on designing spaces that are prescriptive in the types of movement they allow. Dance-makers and choreographers, however, acquire an embodied knowledge of the built environment, better understanding how collective and individual bodies feel and fold into the city. This expertise can be invaluable in the architectural and urban design. A fleeting comment made at the end of the London Lab has remained in my mind: 'what if, alongside sustainability, engineering, and heritage consultants, embodied movement specialists join design teams as consultants at an early stage?' What possibilities could this create for our cities? What new vocabularies, gestures, and lexicons would emerge?

Instead of relying purely on sight and intellect, a common gestural language for architecture and dance would ask us to reimagine design through all our bodily senses.[12] Such embodied knowledge could be utilised to design more equitable, fun, accessible, safe, and dynamic spaces for all, whilst feeding into a process of (un)learning from past spatial experiences and understanding their effect on our presence in the city and access to public space.

Integrating that knowledge into the design practice is not a short-term process. Early on in their training, dancers learn how to be in a room together and how to be in relation to each other. The act of creating and entering into an ensemble means, 'I do not know what it is to be you/like you, but I know you are here'. Architects may need to experience this relational capacity as well. Thanks to experiments like the Movement Forum, we can understand how our bodies feel in different settings, whether that occurs when we listen to emancipatory stories or experience physical limitations, whilst walking, or when we create a new gestural vocabulary through dancing. Although a revelatory performance, encounter or enactment may unearth spatial or societal inequities in the public realm, it will not necessarily lead to better design in the first instance. It can, however, create new ways of occupying space, be that disruptive or compliant, permanent or temporal. We should, therefore, seek to expand the role of who makes the city and collaborate with practitioners who conceive and experience mobility differently, should we want to design spaces that do not limit these possibilities. To do this, our very scripted ways of being must come undone.[13] We must become undisciplined.

12 Karimnia, E. and Kostourou, F. (2021) *Embodying Otherness*.

13 Halberstam, J. (2020), "Jack Halberstam on Wildness, Illegibility and the Commercialization of Desire", *Frieze* [frieze.com/interview/jack-halberstam-wild-things-disorder-of-desire]

Movement I

London

Power and Gender

The theme of the London Lab was provoked by the most recent, yet not the last, events of violence against women in London.[1] Such gender-based power dynamics can be also found in the form of symbolic[2] or non-physical violence within the built environment. Unsurprisingly, these issues are the manifestation of a male-dominated decisions and ambitions shape everyone's access to and safety in public spaces. Their expertise often lacks a real understanding of inequality issues that are felt not only by women, but also by *others*: unrecognised, discriminated, or marginalised bodies in public space. To include others starts by acknowledging *otherness* and considering *othering*, that is the act of doing things differently, embracing non-confirmative ways of seeing and making the city. In the recent Theatrum Mundi edition, *Embodying Otherness*,[3] we addressed this knowledge gap, exploring othering through a choreographic lens. Following suit in the Movement Forum, we expanded on those questions, asking specifically how gender-based power dynamics can be revealed and resisted. By what strategies can public spaces as civic infrastructure be de- or re-gendered? And how can built environment professionals better integrate otherness into spatial design?

Staging [otherness]

The public realm is a platform for recognising others. It is the medium to reflect on and navigate the plurality of bodies, identities, and choices, while sharing space and negotiating personal interactions that vary from attentive togetherness, respect, and care to spontaneous, fleeting encounters, and collective actions. This realisation found itself at the core of the London Lab. Yet finding an available public space to test it was not simple.

After several attempts to host the workshop in the outdoor space of cultural institutions in central London, it became clear that public safety and risk control protocols complicated the process of getting permission, making it almost impossible for us to navigate into a bureaucratic system that manages privately owned public spaces in the city. Our efforts to be granted permission sparked the first questions about power dynamics and how public public spaces truly are. What kinds of activities are allowed, where, for how long, and by whom? They also left us with no choice but to run the workshop in the interior and exterior garden of Groupwork office, which imposed further limitations on the kind of choreographic activities we could plan and accommodate. To counter some of the limitations of the privately owned space, we came up with the idea of 'staging' as a way to temporarily transform the publicness of the space, designing anew the conditions for experimenting with otherness and testing how design may transform our embodied experiences.

Staging was done by à la sauvette architecture collective, inviting the participants to 'party', to feel free, to go wild, and to practise intimacy. The stage was set up at the threshold of 15A Clerkenwell Close

1   71% of women in London have experienced violence in public spaces.

2   Symbolic violence is manifested in the power differential between social groups.

3   Karimnia, E. and Kostourou, F. (2021) *Embodying Otherness*.

building. The light silver curtain à la sauvette hung from the well-preserved façade of the building constituted a 'performing' boundary, one that could stand still in one moment and flow in the air soon after. Whilst affording different atmospheres on each side of the curtain, its movement offered a physical, psychological, and emotional transition between the open and the semi-closed space, the public street and the private pilotis, the visible and the invisible, the exposed and the protected. It provided the spatial conditions to experience otherness and raise awareness of *them* versus *us* in space.

Unlike the in situ experiment by à la sauvette, the stage for the dance artist Sara Wookey and her collaborator Ellie Cosgrove expanded to include a sequence of nearby spaces in the city: a grass field around St James Church, an open space next to St John's Square, inside Smithfield's Market, around the most unusual trees of Smithfield's Rotunda Garden, and finally an open space in the Barbican Estate. The duo saw staging neither as an act of foregrounding the city nor as an attempt to create a deliberate division between us and others, but rather as a possibility for building a relationship with self, others, and the landscape. A different approach was also adopted by fem_arc architecture collective. During the audiowalk, they left the participants to decide and plan their own 'staging' on-the-go as they walked through different places, whilst listening to provocative distanced narratives. The stage was then generated in a flux as a location of attunement, sometimes guided by the audio and sometimes shaped by individual embodied responses to others and to the city.

Navigating [otherness]

Still under the uncertain and agitated atmosphere of the COVID-19 pandemic, 22 people of diverse genders, sexualities, races, and ethnicities gathered together to navigate otherness, regardless of their professional background and prior knowledge in architecture, urbanism, choreography, or dance. To introduce ourselves, Sara Wookey asked us to respond to the question: who am I? 'I am a commuter', 'I am short', 'I am Iranian', 'I am an interrupter'. While standing in a circle on a grass field, we all defined (and redefined) ourselves three times in three rounds in the company of others but far from each other, ensuring there was enough in-between space to comply with the physical distancing rules, but also that we were close enough to listen to each other. While facing others, we saw ourselves, we confronted them, and decided who we wanted to be on that day at that very moment.

Every time this question was asked during the workshop, the answers differed. We felt that *who we are* constantly changed in relation to the situation we were in and the familiarity we had developed. Either seated around a conference table inside the fully glazed office or standing up at the park, the exercise of Who Am I? was a provocation to encounter our self, others, and the city.

Slowly, we started to 'dwell' on the stage, navigating it with others. The navigation was designed through a series of activities, engaging the body – our eyes, hands, feet, pose, and gesture – with the place – its sounds, materials, form, size – and the presence of others. We navigated others through our embodied encounters:

my body,
their body,
her eyes,
the wall,
the boys;

walking,
gazing,
chasing,
following,
interrupting.

The process of navigation began with a brief to follow. The brief was a simple direction for the body, different from a plan. No certain goal or fixed outcome was expected, no special technique was involved. The brief was a direction for our encounters and the navigation was an individual journey experienced collectively through movement and stillness in different places. Our responses to the brief were improvised based on what we encountered, which shaped our knowledge to continue to the next unknown place.

'At least two entities have to arrive to create an encounter, a "bringing forth" in the sense of an occupation [...] The dash in "co-incide" must be highlighted here to avoid turning the shared arrival into a matter of chance. To "co-incide" suggests how different things happen at the same moment, a happening that brings things near to other things, whereby the nearness shapes the shape of each thing'.[4]

The collective iteration of choreographic activities, different from the proper daily use of space, allowed other ways of doing and being in the space, getting comfortable with putting away what we already know about a place and ways of being in the city and exploring new knowledge through encountering. The navigation process turned those places – the park, the square, the market or the pedways of Barbican Estate – into a stage. Navigating otherness was in fact a process of embracing 'co-incident' and unfamiliar encounters.

Walking

Walking is a practice of entering and inhabiting a space; the most routine act of navigating the city. Walking is also a practice to provoke, challenge, and interrupt the expectations, rules, and norms around where we enter and interact in everyday life. In Movement Forum London Lab, we walked as a planned activity but with contingent and improvised responses to whom and to what we encountered; a common activity between different territories, regardless of their publicness. We walked through streets, parks, sidewalks, enclosed markets, and pedways. We could enter and inhabit them regardless of their ownership. Our encounters would have been different if the walk had been taking place in the evening when the same park's gate had been closed off, or if the traffic had been heavy and the market had been open and running, or if it had been a working day for the employees of Groupwork, or if one of us had had mobility issues.

Walking with a group was a socially-engaging practice, navigating collectiveness while respecting different paces and individual choices. It became a collective navigation of co-incident encounters with the liberty of noticing and attuning to things and others differently. For example, not all of us noticed the presence of teenage boys playing chess in the corner of the square where we were moving collectively. With that liberty of navigating other bodies and things around us differently, we adjusted our rhythm and proximity to others, slowing down to read a sign, pausing to take a photo of a shopfront, getting close to eavesdropping or joining others' conversations. Walking became inseparate from the moment we sensed things, a 'bodily intentionality' that 'provides[d] our initial grasp or sense of a situation allowing us to cope with the ongoing flow of experience.'[5]

---

4   Ahmed, S. (2006) *Queer Phenomenology*, p.39.

5   Hale, J. (2017) *Merleau-Ponty for Architects*, pp.13-14, cited in Seamon, D. (2022, forthcoming) "Merleau-Ponty, Environmental Embodiment, and Place: Implications for Architecture and Placemaking" in C. Kakalis (ed), *Embodied Awareness and Space: Body, Agency and Current Practice*.

Listening

Otherness was also navigated through listening; an act to critically think about *other* stories of everyday life in cities. The emancipatory audiowalk was an invitation to individually listen to a series of personal stories and testimonies of conflict for minority bodies, raising questions of privilege and of structural exclusions in the city as a result of its architecture and urban planning. fem_arc's walk was guided by different narrating characters, who invited us to observe details, spaces, and opportunities that we might miss or ignore otherwise in everyday walking, and to become aware of, inspired by, and also attentive to others, either in distance or around us, while noticing our own position. We were also invited to welcome stillness and expansion in the space. A rest in walking allowed our bodies for a moment to attune to our immediate surroundings and to interrupt and dismantle the norms about *who* is visible and exposed in public space and what kind of activities are expected from us.

Landscaping

We also performed a series of improvised responses to the architecturally robust pedways of the Barbican Estate. Our presence and responses to the architectural elements highlighted the affordances of the landscape. Each response was an individual choice, followed by an effort to navigate the landscape to detect not a proper functional opportunity, but rather a structure that supports embodied explorations. More skilled bodies, such as those of choreographers, experimented more with navigating the architecture. Yet skill was not at the core of this practice; it was a collective improvised act of shaping the landscape.

Partying

The music, the light, and the smoke were set to signal a party, changing the ambience of the pilotis of 15A Clerkenwell Close building, but also that of the street. From the outside, people could hear the music and see the smoke coming out of the entrance from time to time when the curtain was flying with the wind. A few people walking on the street came close to the building, looking at the building's speculative architecture and wondering what was happening. The silver curtain dancing in the air, while the pinkish smoke was blown in and out of the pilotis, signalling a 'party', materialising not a solid entrance gate, but a fluid boundary between two worlds and arousing emotions of curiosity for those outside and emotions of intimacy for those inside.

Provoking [otherness]

'I feel blessed',
'I feel expanded',
'I feel nourished',
'I feel anxious',
'I feel cared for',
'I feel grounded',
'I feel present',
'I feel lost',
'I feel full of imagination',
'I feel connected',
'I feel connected',
'I feel connected',
'I feel strong',
'I feel I belong',
'I feel I'm at the start of a new journey',
'I feel an ending marks the beginning',
'I also feel connected', 'I feel included',
'I feel I have many voices'.

Before the end of the lab, we congregated inside the office, in the same space where we met for the first time, to share our thoughts and experiences of new or different ways of exploring otherness in public space. We started by sharing how we felt, and that sharing was an embodied reflection on the experimental process of navigating otherness combined with that of getting familiar with each other. The choreographic briefs served as a sort of 'infrastructure' for this process, guiding us to learn about our body, its movements, restrictions, and privileges. As a shared journey with different feelings, we reflected on our individual differences and how a city can accommodate these experiences. 'It is perhaps not much about inclusion', as one of the participants said, 'but more about justice.' How can we design just spaces?

We discussed ways of communicating power dynamics in public space, reflecting on those used in both the disciplines of architecture and dance and going beyond categories that we are used to reproduce. The conversation distilled otherness to the notion of othering. We discussed if the expert knowledge of dancers or movement specialists is the missing piece to fill the gap in the city design and architecture. If so, shall we include them in the process of design and consult with them on a project basis? Do we also need to come up with a new, shared lexicon and cross-disciplinary methods and tools that help us acknowledge and understand othering beyond preconceived categorisations? Or shall the team of designers learn to bring their own embodied experiences and stories to the design process for designing other realities? How can we then ensure their experiences are diverse enough to represent otherness?

The participants reflected on these questions while appreciating the design and materiality of the 15A Clerkenwell Close building. During the two-day workshop, otherness was experimented with, provoking us to experience co-incidental encounters by listening to other narratives in the city and letting them guide our presence, our movements, and the shaping of a new landscape that complements the built environment without foregrounding or backgrounding it. The experimental nature of the methods allowed us to extend the experience of public space and otherness beyond the joyful experience of a *flâneur*, while the diversity of the participants' backgrounds, genders, and practices enriched the discussion to include an intersectional understanding of otherness.

Elahe Karimnia

34

Thresholds
[Sara Wookey]

The concern Theatrum Mundi prompted for the London event was 'power dynamics' and ways they can be abstracted and incarnated, revealed and resisted. My collaborator, Ellie Cosgrove, and I began thinking about this through interdisciplinary practice and choreographic thinking, understanding *care* as relevant, but perhaps challenging to the idea of *power*. We were interested in an inherent way power feels in the body in relation to spaces of the city, rather than through a *knowing* of what power means. We reformulated the framing question to: how can new forms of interdisciplinarity between city-making and dance-making help engender care for ourselves, the city, and each other?

I will walk you through the choreography of the event and reflect on the different approaches we tested to move in and with oneself, the city, and each other by using the theories and methodologies of expanded choreographic practices. By expanded choreographic practices I am referring to practices of human movement and public space that are informed by techniques learned in dance; techniques that concern social-spatial relations and group dynamics. In considering choreographic practice as a method for trying out different organisational systems of movement, time,

and space, we collaboratively designed a score or series of prompts for people to take up, invent within, and feedback on ideas around power. My aim is to bring you, the reader, into a feeling of the day and of spaces of encounter with self, city, and each other in the hope it might both enlighten considerations of what power is through a consideration of how the city feels to our bodies as we move through its spaces, as well as inspire you to pick up the score and try it out on your own or with others in shared public spaces where you live.

Part of the invitation on offer are tools for engagement that are borrowed from choreographic practices. These include *warming up for the city* – concept developed in collaboration with artist Sara Daleiden in Los Angeles in 2015 – to prepare us physically, mentally, and emotionally for entering a city and, more recently, for returning to the public space post-pandemic. Approaches borrowed from choreographic practice encourage easy-to-learn movements that engage the body, allowing it to be more flexible, agile, and strong, and lead to a greater sense of safety and empowerment in tackling the pressures, concerns, and fears of returning to public spaces.

I am   Begin by walking and say to yourself or another – if accompanied – 'I am (*fill in the blank*) when experiencing the city'. This suggests ways of perceiving the city through your individual lenses, experiences and perceptions. You might then repeat to yourself or your companion, 'I am (*fill in the blank)*' and repeat this back and forth for a few minutes, allowing the noun to shift and change or stay the same.

Warm up   In warming up for exploring the city there are a few movements that can be useful. Consider the feet and hands first and engage in circling actions or flexing and extending as ways to warm up the joints for movement. Other actions might be turning the head from side to side as if saying 'no' or when watching for cars when crossing the street. What do you see and how does what you see resonate as a sensation or feeling in the body? Where might your eyes be drawn to and what associations does that conjure in your physical self?

Circular dance (relating to site)   Invite a circular, non-linear walking path to emerge in a space that is both spacious and safe for moving in. You might seek out architecture that suggests circular patterns. Notice the contrast of curved walking paths in places where angles and linearity dominate. How does this feel?

As you leave this and continue to walk, consider the sensation of your feet on the ground as you walk.

Going inside (relating to self)   Find a place to pause and start to trace a line of awareness mentally from your feet to the top of your head. Notice how it feels internally; where places feel easy and flowing, where there may be tension or stuck places. Witness without judgement. As if saying 'hello' to your interior body.

When you are finished, invite acts of resting in the space before leaving. This might be standing or sitting or slow walking. How might you bring restfulness into your experience?

The portal (relating to the city)   Find a place where you can imagine it as being a portal to some other space. This might be a street, a path, a park, or other space that could transform your experience from being one thing into something else. Use your imagination, as the physical structure is less important than the idea of a portal.

Either with your hand or in your mind, draw an entryway or doorway to your portal and step through it. Walk forward in silence and when you get to the end of the road, pathway or park stop, look back to where you came from, and sense how things may have changed in the way you experience the other side of this imagined portal.

Whether on your own or with a companion, find a space where you can practice subtle movements such as standing and sitting. Mark out in your mind a space in which you will move. Be clear about where the edges of this landscape are. It can be a small, medium, or large area. Step into it on your own, or one at a time if with others, and spontaneously choose where to stand or sit, and for how long. Also notice your spatial/social relationship to others in the space. What kind of compositions of people and space emerge and what role do you play in shaping it?

Writing and/or discussing   Return to the theme of power and reflect back to the beginning when you repeated the 'I am' statements. How do you feel now and has your experience of who you are in the city remained intact or has it changed in any way?

Bring the thoughts and/or discussion back to an understanding of the site, self, and each other. In what ways do you consider how different experiences brought up different sets of relations across these three elements? How might you express that in words?

To conclude   The aim in this invitation is for you, the reader, to engage with the city through an embodied experience and to feel the care for self, the city, and each other. In this way we can begin to discuss larger issues of power – as prompted by Theatrum Mundi – by asking ourselves how we feel in certain situations within the built environment. One memorable experience we had on our walk through London was when we practised circular walking in an area where a row of men were playing chess games. Our predominantly female group-circling felt as a counterpoint – as in a dance – to the linear aligning of the group of men. By being in a group performing these circular walking patterns I felt safe, connected, and visible. Having been alone and not engaged in such an activity, my sense is I would have felt more disconnected and possibly less safe and visible.

This project was informed by my practice and research both of which are based in exploring the knowledge of dancers and choreographers, and the role of artists in society. The project was also informed by the work of Ellie Cosgrove on inclusive urbanisation, particularly with respect to gender and just climate transition. For both of us, this was an opportunity to challenge ways that movement through and with the city might prompt modes of being and doing that are sensitive to our social-spatial relations, and poetically complicate the idea of power in public space.

Confronting our own assumptions
[fem_arc | Lara Stöhlmacher]

'*I walk because it confers – or restores – a feeling of place-ness. I walk because, somehow, it's like reading. You're privy to these lives and conversations that have nothing to do with yours, but you can eavesdrop on them. Sometimes it's overcrowded; sometimes the voices are too loud. But there is always companionship. You are not alone. You walk in the city side by side with the living and the dead*'.[1]

1   Elkin, L. (2017) *Flaneuse - Women Walk the City in Paris, New York, Tokyo, Venice and London*, p. 26.

fem_arc collective started to look into walking in cities in 2020, and in particular at the absent figure of the *flâneuse*, when the curators of 'A Feminist Perspective for Berlin Today! What could a non-sexist city look like?' asked us to do a guided tour for their exhibition. They invited us to visit buildings in Berlin that respond to Dolores Hayden's influential essay with the same title.[1] Hayden had rightly criticised how cities were built around the needs of family models with a traditionally gendered division of labour. We thought that, although still incredibly relevant today, this exclusive focus on reproductive labour and the built spaces that contain it, did not reflect well on the many ways in which gender-related power dynamics shaped our own use and experience of space. Our collective at that point had six members, and each of us already had a range of individual perspectives to bring to the discussion that were much more nuanced and shifted depending on the context. So, we sought a tool that could help push beyond static notions of space and sexism, reflecting on mechanisms of oppression and emancipation; a performative tool that would allow us to experience with our whole bodies how these different mechanisms manifest themselves in urban space as well as in individual experiences, and that could demonstrate the simultaneity and diversity of our jointly composed realities in a relatable way.

The fact that the pandemic had suddenly and greatly reduced our habitual uses of public spaces to mainly walking and that our communication had become largely digital, opened new perspectives on the task for us. If we were to make our mobile phones our walking partner, we could carry quite different voices along with us. Without geographical limitations, we could reach out to and involve a much wider audience. So, who did we want to take for a walk and let bring us closer to a spatial practice that responds to, confronts or countervails marginalisations?

For over two years now, we have been collecting stories about emancipatory spatial practices told by artists, activists, and architects in European cities. We have gradually been integrating these stories into audiowalks, slowly informing and expanding our research on the topic, which remains ambiguously defined today. What the interlocutors have in common is that they invite participants of the resulting audiowalk series F_WALKS to experience strategies for creating more equitable spaces based on lived experiences.

---

1   Hayden, D. (1980) "What Would a Non-Sexist City Be Like? Speculations on Housing, Urban Design, and Human Work". *Signs*, 5(3): 170–87.

Naomi Boima, for example, talks about the impact street names, stemming from colonial times, have on racialised bodies, and how she frees herself from agonising discussions about replacing those names. Sarnt Utamachote from un.thai.tled, a collective of Thai creatives in Berlin, recounts how Southeast Asian communities turned a Prussian park in Berlin into a pivotal place for community exchange. In a performative experiment, Kerstin Honeit invites bodies perceived as female to claim space without giving in to the reflex to justify their presence. And in London, Jos Boys and Zoe Partington from the Disordinary Architecture Project share teaching methods that take the experience of diverse bodies as a starting point to rethink spatial justice. Unequal power dynamics based on gender are more or less present in all these stories, but the focus is on transformational strategies that have emerged from far more diverse forms of marginalisation.

By the time we visited Theatrum Mundi's Movement Forum in London, the Guiding voiceS audiowalk had been downloaded more than two thousand times and we had performed it together with groups in several cities, collecting a new perspective from each site. The workshop in London also took place almost exactly one year after our first Guiding voice performance, a suitable occasion to confront our initial motivations with new experiences. The following fragments are excerpts partly from the audiowalk's sound files and partly from the conversations these walks prompted. These reflections remain incomplete. They are situated and may contradict each other, and, most importantly, they will continue to evolve with every new walk and every new encounter in response to the question: Can listening become a collective spatial practice?

Guiding voice [00:01:36] 'As you begin moving, start at a slower pace than usual, notice the sensations while you are moving: heaviness, lightness, pressure, tingling, energy, even pain if it's present...'

Audiowalk participant 1, London 'I remember that, for a long time you just use half of your body... because the other side you have to kind of hold from this offence. In everyday life, we just go through so many awful places. And yet we can accept this. Because this is how it is. It's just so ridiculous, though, why we don't think about what's wrong; why we learned to ignore it.'

Guiding voice [00:02:25] '...We understand listening as a critical practice, an active practice that develops and enhances awareness. Listening, understood as a point of departure for relational processes and a point of departure for a conversation, for yourself and with others. What can listening to other people's stories do with us? How can we bring a spatial and collective aspect to listening? Can listening be understood as a collective spatial practice?'

'...And then for me, the word discipline is the worst enemy. Because you enclose yourself: This is my territory. This is what we do. So, there's already a blockage in the conversation. I hate the word disciplinary...'

Against the dominance of the visual in architecture, our collective has been experimenting for some time with non-visual representations of spaces, especially with formats for active listening. In the audiowalk, we try to engage the audience in non-habitual enactments and the uncovering of previously unnoticed functions of spaces through listening and moving. And yet, despite having performed many iterations of the same walk, the exchange we had with dance professionals in London suddenly made me aware of how inept my language and senses still were at grasping the full scope of the embodied part of this practice.

'...As dancers we kind of learn how to be in the room together. We practise with others, we train together... So, there's a real kind of social understanding. I'm very aware, when I'm in a dance piece, of where everybody else is in the space, even if I'm not looking at them... There's something about relationality. It's not just a dancer who knows how to be in their body, in that individual, but it is in relationship to others. And I don't know how to name that but there is something, I think, that we desperately need, to be comfortable in the room together. Even if we don't understand another's experiences, we can be together in space and create a sense of shared collective value...'

'...At the end of the day, your body experiences on its own. That's why I think the more you open up to discussions like this, trying, if possible, to expand your own experiences, by listening to others' experiences, by exposing yourselves to other possibilities... the more you can understand and accommodate some of that experience, which, otherwise, you might not have been able to actually embody.'

Guiding voice [00:03:33] 'Where are you now? Keep moving. Do you see people around you? Many of them or just a few? Maybe no one at all? Who is visible on the streets? Who isn't?'

The audiowalk collects perspectives that are oftentimes invisible, inaudible, and overlooked in city planning. Yet, we are aware that our effort only captures a fraction of the lived experiences in cities – not to forget what happens beyond these. With such a nonrepresentative sample, it is probably too early to claim our role in platforming the marginalised and unheard voices. So, when we talk about representing the embodied experiences of the collective, who is still missing from that?

Audiowalk participant 1, Berlin '...When we use other people's stories in our work, we are always mindful to treat them respectfully and treat their stories respectfully too. We also ask ourselves how we can retroactively give back to the people who have shared their experiences with us.'

Audiowalk participant 5, London '...if you are sitting at the table, having a position of power, obviously you are only able to ever judge something from your own positionality. But... what if there's something that is about expanding the imagination, so that you can imagine saying: Okay, there was something here that I don't know about. My imagination is big enough to know that I don't know about this thing. Then I'm going to kind of have to get some information about this thing. But then if the person you're talking to also knows that there's a space in their imagination that they don't know about, that's when the new ideas come about. So, I think we have to be a little bit wary about saying: "There's a group of people who have all the answers." [...] I think there's something really important about kind of opening up possibilities, of imagining together. For me, the question is: What is that technique? What can that bring about?'

Although the audiowalk puts focus on listening, developing awareness of our own bodies in space is not achieved by the mere means of listening alone. In fact, it seems to happen – quite effortlessly – on the occasion of collective seeing, listening, and doing. It is precisely this immersive and embodied access to others' experiences, views, and recollections that makes a difference. It is the interruption, amplification, articulation, and dismissal of our own habitual performances when these are exposed to otherness.

Guiding voice [00:28:00] '...we would like to invite you to do the opposite, and to move with us, as slowly as you can. Focus on the space between your footsteps... To look for details that we might miss otherwise. It's not important where we arrive to at the end. Let's just start moving ... but veeeery slowly.'

Audiowalk participant, Copenhagen '...We only curate the walk and this doesn't mean we direct, know, or even anticipate what other participants will experience. I did the audio walk several times, sometimes in the same area. Each time I discovered different things, some of which had to do with my moods and thoughts of the day, others with the other people and things that were present that day.'

Audiowalk participant 6, London '...one of the most moving parts for me, from that audio, was when they were starting to talk about disability and inclusion. They were saying: "Let's not use inclusion, but let's use justice". Powerful. We can make certain assumptions, and we can put things into categories, but.... I have to be so mindful that even if a person self-identifies as something, I can't place any assumptions on what that might mean not only to them, but to me as well.'

As critical architects, our task can't be to reduce the complexity of urban experience to normative categories to make it easier for us to design for and with it. Equitable spaces won't be achieved by guidance, but spatial justice is a matter of maximising solidarity through recurring negotiations. In the London lab, we talked about the ephemerality of our movements in contrast to the permanence of built spaces. If our movements are ephemeral then the realisations, feelings, and other ways of being that we experience through these movements, are also ephemeral. To keep them from fading away, we must get into the habit of practising regularly.

Embodied openness
[Mahsa Alami Fariman]

Can performance transform the prefigured perception and categorisation of female identity within the built environment?

The question popped into my head when I found myself in 15A Clerkenwell Close in central London. The architects of the building overturned its demolition order and allowed, instead, a 'surprise of unpredicted natural finishes to occur'.[1] In that very space of resistance, I joined a group of choreographers and spatial practitioners to re-think the process of self-identification in the built environment through performance. This was particularly important for me. Being a woman and growing up in a restricted socio-political context, my body had learned to overcome certain societal norms, cultural codes, and political restrictions while walking, talking, laughing, and being in the city. But in that space and with that question in mind, I felt immediately eager to focus on my female identity to embody resistance through performance.

After reaching the Barbican Estate, I took on the metaphor of *openness* as a tool to subvert the effects of such restrictive conventions; however, not through the manipulation of socio-political codes, but by corporealising openness.[2] Surrounded by a brutal architecture that itself opposes conventional ideas of beauty, I decided to perform an ordinary movement in a way that is not usually socially and culturally accepted for women in my country. I laid down, expanded my body, and spread my arms to welcome the force of the built environment, whilst facing fearfully towards the forty-four-storey high Shakespeare Tower above me. It was an intentional and performative act of disobedience. With my arms and legs wide open, my so-called feminine, soft, fragile, and delicate body was now standing against the rough, brutal, masculine, and coarse tower.

With this act of mine, the south terrace of the complex, surrounded by the Barbican towers, transformed into a stage, where my individual body started negotiating its power-relation to the architecture and the presence of others. Actively positioning my body in such an unconventional yet open way against the concrete robust built environment, advocated for a process of both becoming open to new possibilities and changing, transforming, and redefining the historically accepted female identity.

1   Khanchandani, P. (2019) "Amin Taha on 15 Clerkenwell Close, his home and studio threatened with demolition", *ICON* [iconeye.com/architecture/architecture-news/amin-taha-interview-clerkenwell-close-icon-minds]

2   Hanson, J. (2007) "Drag Kinging: Embodied Acts and Acts of Embodiment". *Body & Society*, 13(1): 61-106.

All that glitters is not gold
[Adam Moore]

Following our collective encounter intervening in the expansive and labyrinthine Brutalist architecture of the Barbican, our conversation naturally flowed into examining how dance and people working with dance – like myself – can operate in different spaces. Comparing outdoor spaces, like the docks, with places and buildings designed specifically for dancing, raised questions about the differences in dance-making potential when a building's design fails to meet the specific needs of a dancer. It also brought to the fore design considerations that can be sometimes overlooked in the making of buildings and cities and which influence how hospitable their spaces can be for their users.

Designed by Herzog and de Meuron in collaboration with visual artist Michael Craig-Martin, the Trinity Laban Conservatoire of Dance (2003) seems as contemporary as its counterpart, the Conservatoire of Music at King Charles Court – formerly the Royal Hospital for Seamen (1694-1869) before becoming the Royal Naval College (1873-1997), designed by Sir Christopher Wren – is historic. The Laban Centre gleams on bright days, slicing through the blue sky, skating across the green grass that surrounds it, with blades of light ricocheting forcefully. It is impressive to behold. From outside it seems like it could be a contemporary dance conservatoire. Inside, underfoot in all communal areas is a tough concrete that on relentless days of classes takes its toll on the body. Something softer might have been more forgiving and welcoming, and, overall, more aligned with the physically exerted body. The large glass doors into and out of each studio allow you to see out and be seen, but the windows in almost every studio are opaque. Floor to ceiling, the grey glass is oppressive, not only because

you cannot see out, but because despite the extraordinary glass to wall ratio, there are no windows that open. The walls are grey; the floor too. Not quite a sensory deprivation but rather an overstimulation of neutralising grey which feels jarring, dreary, and at odds with the ease that a body needs in order to dance. What if we were to consider the light conditions, the external visibility, the access to fresh air and how this circulates through a building, the colour, and the texture of the materials? Those ecological and sensorial qualities that cultivate a greater degree of hospitality, and enable one to *be*, rather than *question* their being when confronted with such challenging architectural conditions. Behind its crisply choreographed exterior, the Laban building is not what it seems.

Compromising and negotiating will always be necessary when designing spaces suitable for as many as possible. For there is no such thing as a *standard* body with a *standard* size, height, weight, gender, race, sexual orientation, and standard needs. Instead, there are intersectional bodies with differentiated embodied experiences and perspectives, who seek to inhabit and simply be in spaces without having to constantly adjust to them. And there are also ecological and sensorial qualities afforded in the design of things which determine these experiences. A reflexive evaluation of the design quality balances aesthetics with function, inclusivity, and physical accessibility. Multiplicity of embodied subjectivities is essential in the process of synthesising, designing, and building cities, if we want the places where we live and belong to reflect our multi-dimensional other species; a concern which is critical for our mutual sustainability.

Rehearsing for the city
[Eloise Maltby Maland]

On the nineteenth September 2021
I listened to fem_arc's audio walk
with Kerstin Honeit instructing me to
squat a space
to claim it with my presence
I walked through a park
my body expanding
trying to hold the space
a tense discomfort rising

I begin slowly
to recognise the discomfort
that I couldn't understand at the time
how I couldn't hold my position for the
three minutes
the flutters rushing through my body
the repeated wish running through my
mind
for nobody to pass by
for nobody to witness my body
in this posture of claiming
giving in
and releasing my posture
my body letting out a sigh of relief

my body letting out a sigh of relief
as this posture
doesn't sit easily on my skin

I am used to continuously

shifting my shoulders, neck, chin,
elbows
in relation with the city
a necessary
response to
its spatial codes
norms and languages
embedded in my body

moving as strategy

a learnt choreography
sticky with rehearsed practice.

As we rehearse
our relationships with the city,

how do spatial choreographies
become

imprinted in our bodies?

How can new

postures
of presence

softly begin to rehearse

a different
choreography

for the city?

Five days before I sit to write this
many weeks after hearing
Kerstin Honeit's
voice

I walked through a park
my body contracting
the light dimming
a group of boys
children
shifting their weight into their back legs
and throwing apples and stones at us
us – three female bodies

gravel in our hair

they threw words as hard as stones
'perras, bolleras, bitches, dykes'
exposing the ingrained

embedded

inherited fabrics of power
through

the stones and apples
of children

as they

moved as one body

a learnt choreography
as if rehearsed
knowing
with a certainty
that their bodies
in that space and time
had a power over
our bodies.

Eye, I: Revisiting the King's Arms
[Lee Campbell]

In an interview with Tim Kirk for his *Two Zero Q: 20 Questions with Interesting People from the LGBT community and friends* podcast in July 2020, he asked me to describe a seemingly overwhelming task or difficult situation I had to overcome in the past. Having realised I was gay in my mid-late teens in the mid 1990s, a personal challenge was stepping inside a gay bar for the first time. My feelings just before going into London's The King's Arms pub in Soho echoed those that Tim shared: 'I wanted to experience the culture, the life, the very first pulse-stopping-heart-in-my-throat time in a gay bar'. Once inside, no truer words than these could be found: 'Gay men tend to be a very ocular focused society: we look and when we like what we see, we look again... but we are cruising you to see if you cruise me back and if we are cruising each other then I know that I am desirable'.[1]

In The King's Arms, I first discovered that bears and cubs don't just live in the forest. As a gay man in the early 2000s in London, I felt at home amongst men who looked like me, whose bodies were like mine. I found men with this body type very desirable, and likewise I wanted men to find my body sexy and attractive. I was putting myself on sale; wanted to get myself 'sold', and not left on the shelf. But I soon learned that there were power relations and antagonisms, processes of inclusion, and exclusion; gay men can exclude, leave you outside in the cold as quick as they can include and convivially welcome. I was told I was too slim to be a 'bear and too fat to be a 'cub'. So where do I go?

Theatrum Mundi's workshop in London in September 2021 prompted me to revisit The King's Arms and write a short poem with accompanying poetry film:[2]

1   *Beauty Before Age: Growing Older in Gay Culture* (1997) Film directed by Johnny Symons.

2   *Bears With Bananas And Bubbles In Their Boxers* (2022) Film directed by Lee Campbell, *FilmFreeway* [filmfreeway.com/bearswithbananasandbubblesintheirboxers]

I remember my first time in The King's Arms pub
Where I soon learnt gay men are labelled 'bear' or 'cub'

Eye, I, eye, I
Am I
too fat to be a cub, too slim to be a bear?

It seems bigger the butt the better, it's true
And if a guy has more than eight inches, you lucky boy you
Gays may lie but believe me they squirm
If the snake in a guy's Calvin's is the size of a worm

Surely it's time to turn the tables
on gay male body shaming and this obsession with labels?
Men seeing and being seen. Brother to brother
But their labelling whilst cruising is bruising each other
Guys out cruising, putting themselves on sale
Cheapening and reducing themselves in this marketplace hell
Like customers in shops, cruisers want satisfaction
How far will they go to get some action?
The King's Arms in the '90s, a cocktail of body labels and lying
You would soon learn cruising, like shopping, is an experience so unsatisfying

Guys, young and old, always bend the truth
Daddies like twinks 'cos they like the smell of their youth
Whilst embellishing the facts to make themselves
          more desirable
To get that all important hook-up, to make themselves feel
          more hireable
To make their bulges look bigger to admiring silver foxes
Bears stuffing bananas down the front of their Calvin Klein boxers
Making their butts look bigger with plastic bubble wrap
Imagine the pain these guys felt if they needed to crap

Daddies going berserk seeing them twerk
I doubt if they care these butts are just bubble wrap air

Burst the bubbles, ease the troubles
Let's build a love for our own bodies out of the rubble

Movement II

Paris

Wildness and Queer Counter-Publics

The Movement Forum Paris Lab brought together voguing, parasitic reading, and a woodland installation to explore 'wild' movement. It asked: What would it mean to invite true wildness into central urban public spaces? What solidarities can be forged between marginalised forms of both human and non-human life? How do they create spaces for flourishing and transgression of the controls that urban regulation attempts to impose?

Wildness imagined and found

These questions were raised for me by a curious paradox between the way *wild* nature is described by the City of Paris in its aim to green the city centre, and my own experience of the already-existing wild spaces located at the city fringes. The current Mayor of Paris, Anne Hidalgo, has spoken of creating 'urban forests' in key public spaces, ripping up concrete and stone to create dense clusters of trees, supporting biodiversity and fighting against the 'heat island' effect of hard-surfaced spaces in this densest city of Europe. The utopian architectural renders distributed to communicate this vision have shown a grove of trees outside Paris's City Hall, with dappled shade and meadow-like grass merging seamlessly into the surrounding paving stones, interspersed with benches and streetlights. While butterflies flit, casual strollers pass through; their passage unhindered by the trees that form a pleasant backdrop to the kinds of public life that look much the same way as they would in any urban square.

Seeing this image over the last couple of years, I couldn't help feeling a certain cognitive dissonance with my experience of the existing woodlands on Paris's fringe. As a new Parisian in the summer of 2020, seeking connection with the city's queer community, I headed deep into the woods of Vincennes (*Bois de Vincennes*) on the border of Paris and its surrounding suburbs. I was following the promise of a party I had seen being discussed on a private Facebook group, which had been established to organise temporary spaces of queer gathering, while the city's nightclubs remained closed. On a hot summer's night, having cycled as far as smooth paths through the woods would take me, I found myself pushing my bike through piles of leaves, branches catching on the wheels, tripping over roots, following a pin on a map without any of the usual urban landmarks that would normally guide me. I expected little more than a small gathering of people around a loud speaker, but it turned out to be much more than this: a mass of queer bodies pressing together, dancing, and touching, more or less clothed. And as the night got deeper, I slowly discovered an alternate reality of raves dotted through the woods, pulsating with lights and music, organised for no other reason than the love of assembling, reminding me of the free parties I hunted across the countryside near my childhood home at the ages of seventeen and eighteen.

This night changed my sense of queer nightlife in Paris, *how* and *where* I could find it. Not that the rules are technically different in the woods than in any other of the city's open public spaces. But rather that they create a shadowy, permissive zone where rules are more easily bent, bodies can be freer, music can be louder. In the dense, illuminated fabric of the city, different flows keep to their lanes: cars drive on the street, pedestrians walk on the pavement, dancing happens in the nightclub; different rhythms of movement are regulated and designed for. However, the woods allow for wilder mobility, where a zone for a party is not predetermined but claimed temporarily, transformed through the act of dancing, and then left in its original form. Same for a picnic, but also for a bed for momentary lovers, or a makeshift shelter for a sexworker or an unhoused person, all of which are common in the woods of Boulogne and Vincennes. So, when seeing those renderings of Hidalgo's proposed urban forests, I wondered: what kind of happenings did the city government imagine amongst those trees, and how did they plan to stop instances of life that fall outside the boundaries? Is human wildness also invited in their proposal of bringing back non-human 'wildness'?

Of course, things are not really that simple, nor are the woods so innocent. For they ultimately do not offer the same freedom to everyone, as we will see. So, can we learn from queer, decolonial, and political readings of the wilds to cultivate justice in the mobilities that become possible amongst the trees?

Decolonial wilds

When I proposed to the performer, scholar, and activist Habibitch to present their performance-lecture Decolonising the Dancefloor in the *Bois de Vincennes*, I thought they might find it a little strange. But their response took me by surprise: 'I'd love to do that. I need to exorcise the woods of their evils, for the sake of my ancestors.' I had imagined the woods as a space for hedonistic freedom, but Habibitch's Algerian heritage connects them to a different history. The woods are not the same for everybody. They were in fact the site of two colonial exhibitions in the early 20th century – where indigenous people from across France's empire had been exhibited. What appears now, then, as a patch of virgin, autonomous nature within the city has also been the ground on which brutal, racist

human trafficking had been 'celebrated'. Is letting the vestiges of the colonial exhibition be taken over by wild growth, until they become picturesque ruins, a way of greenwashing their history and invisibilising the suffering they brought about? Does this come at odds with the bucolic image of the woods? What politics are hidden amongst the trees?

Political scientist Malcolm Ferdinand, in the book *Decolonial Ecology*,[1] asks us to consider from whose perspective the 'ecologically beneficial' is imagined. He critiques the colonial framework of contemporary ecology imposed on the Caribbean by countries of the Global North in the guise of aid. Reforestation projects, he argues, attempt to 'recreate' virgin nature, devoid of human presence, where the pre-colonial reality is that human and non-human cultures were contingent and inseparable. As Soft Agency's architect and curator Rosario Talevi pointed out in the discussion that followed her workshop in the Paris Lab, Germany allows so-called polluted nature to be destroyed in urban development, as long as it is replaced with 'better', cleaner nature. This moral hierarchy of natures that places a higher value on that which is seen to be 'free' from the pollution of the human, is also critiqued by urban planner Marion Waller in her book *Artefacts Naturels* [*Natural Artefacts*],[2] as she argues for a social and inclusive mode of natural reparation. Malcolm Ferdinand describes the clearing of indigenous forests in the Caribbean, with all of their human and non-human entanglements, to make way for plantations, as one of the foundational acts of colonialism and therefore of modern capitalism. We see the

1   Malcom, F. (2021) *Decolonial Ecology: Thinking from the Caribbean World*.

2   Marion. W. (2016) *Artefacts naturels : Nature, réparation, responsabilité*.

same process now within European cities, as both capitalist urban redevelopment and centralised political power look to 'clear' the wild and overgrown to smooth the way for development and tourism. In Paris, for example, environmentalist Jennifer Foster describes how the Petite Ceinture, a decommissioned rail line circling the capital, was 'cleared' of informal inhabitations for homeless migrants and guerrilla gardening and farming to create a 'better' and more 'accessible' kind of managed wild space for urban hikers and dog walkers.[3]

Gender theorist Jack Halberstam critiques the same colonial view of wildness, drawing attention to its othering of 'unnatural' queer and trans bodies that 'go against' nature. For him, this colonial imaginary has driven the violent suppression of indigenous cultures, which have been perceived as socially and sexually deviant in nature – including non-binary genders, shamanisms, and ecological practices belonging to many pre-colonial societies.[4] But if we think of queerness as a set of embodied mobilities – in dance, in gesture, in gathering, in shifting the body through gender spectrums, in ways of seeking intimacy and moving towards desire – rewilding, then, as it is mobilised in contemporary ecology and urban planning, is more about stilling these movements than inviting them. It assumes the perspective of an able, cisgendered, heterosexual body for a version of human and ecological health that is based on public activities affirmed as 'healthy': hiking, enjoying nature. As queer ecologist Cy Lecerf Maulpoix argues; 'behind the condemnation of cruising spots in so-called 'natural' territories, hides without doubt reactivated forms of exclusion of deviant sexualities, along with

a hygienist conception of nature'.[5] If the 'wilds' as spaces are to avoid becoming tools for a further marginalisation, rewilding as a process must become a cultivation of political conditions for queer embodiment, encounter, and wholeness. So, what kind of politics can rewilding put into action?

Autonomous wilds

It turned out that, after all, the city is not deep enough to sustain a forest. The flagship project at Paris's City Hall has been quietly cancelled, citing complications with the densely-packed urban soil. We want trees for their leaves and branches but we clearly don't think enough about their roots, as philosopher Emmanuele Coccia asks us to. The interconnected root systems of forests need more space than can be found in a subterranean urban world already colonised by human infrastructure. This raises a doubt as to whether wild space can really be incorporated into cities, and what kind of politics would make this possible.

As many gay men know, finding a cruising ground – mostly gay male spaces, as geographer Matthew Gandy suggests – usually takes some work. It might be the furthest point of a coastal path from the last urban bus stop, or through the dense overgrowth at the edge of a park, on the steep paths clinging to the side of a hilltop park, or in the centre of a labyrinth of hedges. Out of need for safety and invisibility, cruising happens in spaces you move 'to' rather than 'through'. As a result, cruising zones are ableist spaces, where idealised able bodies gain both easiest access and most attention.

Wild, untended nature, which is often the setting for cruising, raises a similar conundrum. It can be found at the edges

3   Foster, F. (2014) "Hiding in Plain View: Vacancy and Prospect in Paris' Petite Ceinture". *Cities*, 40(B): 124–32.

4   Halberstam, J. (2020) *Wild Things: The Disorder of Desire*.

5   Maulpoix, C.L. (2021) *Écologies déviantes: voyage en terres queers*: 236 [author's translation].

of cities, or along edges within them, on motorway verges or abandoned railway lines, growing on abandoned plots closed off by barriers. It thrives when it is left alone – like cruising – off-centre from the 'beaten tracks' of urban mobility. In this sense, cruising and the wilds are kinds of counter-public, or even anti-public, at least in relation to the limited kind of publicness imagined in Hidalgo's woods, where flows of tourists and shoppers are unhindered by tangled roots. What happens when these liminal spaces within or at the edge of cities get noticed? The story of the Petite Ceinture is once again revealing: along with other 'illicit' uses, the rail line and its thick overgrowth offered hidden places for sexual encounters, something that is no longer possible in its new 'public' form. Wildlife is protected, yet the human forms of wildness that coexisted with them are pushed out in the process.

Responding to this normative agenda, curator Gilly Tarjevsky of Soft Agency, in a presentation for the CSM Forest School in January 2022, argued that rewilding must enact a challenge to the legal and political structures governing the way spaces are made and maintained.[6] Marion Waller offers language that could mobilise this challenge: non-human life, she reminds us, always possesses the capacity for autonomy, even if it is not always able to practice it.[7] Plants taken out of the ecosystems in which they can subsist become reliant on human care. Perhaps, therefore, we should be talking about autonomy rather than wildness, in ways that encompass both human cultures and the ability of plants to grow and reproduce without intervention. Urban rewilding, then, could be asserted as an affirmation of the possibility for things to co-exist whilst remaining self-sustaining, visible but left alone, with an acknowledgment that this flourishing happens in an ecosystem of support infrastructures.

Elahe Karimnia, in the workshop discussion, raised a tension in this idea. Are the conditions of human and non-human autonomy in cities always compatible? The tangled, wild ground of the woods of Vincennes do not allow for independent access for those with limited mobility, and the darkness of the night there feels unsafe for those habituated to the threat of cispatriarchal violence. But we know that infrastructures for human safety and access – bright lighting and smooth asphalt pathways – interfere with the mobility of non-human life, by interrupting ecological continuities and disorienting navigational capacities. How can, then, urban designers prioritise when the mobility of humans and non-humans are in conflict? In the short term, the answer is unclear. But more broadly, this problem highlights the importance of connecting struggles. Perhaps, if, instead of using technologies for control and profit, these were made available as creative tools for new forms of disabled mobility[8] we could live in knottier, darker, and wilder cities without the need to mitigate the threat of male violence.

Practising wildness

So how, while working towards these aims, can we stage wildness in the city? In studies of Berlin's urban ecology, geographer Sandra Jasper warns of the gentrification of nature, as an image of wildness that becomes decoupled from the autonomy that enacts it.[9] I see the same warning in Habibitch's call

6   Central Saint Martins (2022) *The Forest School Talks: NatureCulture*, 2022 [https://www.youtube.com/watch?v=j6gu1qbdUIA]

7   Waller, *Artefacts naturels*.

8   Hamraie, A. and Fritsch, K. (2019) "Crip Technoscience Manifesto". *Catalyst: Feminism, Theory, Technoscience*, 5(1): 1–33.

9   Jasper, S. (2021) "Traversing Wastelands: Reflections on an Abandoned Railway Yard" in C. O'Callaghan

to Decolonise the Dancefloor, presented in the Paris Lab and in this edition. Performing a history of vogue as a critical strategy for visibility and survival developed by queer people marginalised within a broader LGBTQI+ community due to their race, Habibitch call out the appropriation of this dance form by white people as a disposable accessory of cultural awareness. When cultures are transformed from expressions of solidarity and collective joy, embedded in communities and places, to symbols that can be exchanged to allow value to be extracted from those places, this is also gentrification. In ecology, the concept of succession describes the ability of plants to grow from one generation to the next via their own reproductive processes, and the implicit environmental preferences expressed through these. Similarly, human wildness happens when expressions of life can flourish along chosen paths, without being constrained to appropriate times and spaces, or mined for the value they can offer to others. As Barbara Araque suggested in the Paris Lab discussion, by seeking ancestral mythologies and connections to nature that have existed in every part of the earth, we can find our own ways to practise wildness, drawing from our own chains of cultural succession, without appropriating cultures in which we do not have a stake. In cities like London and Paris, as Araque pointed out, we only have to look back as far as the medieval era to find households constituted across species, non-nuclear families, matriarchal societies, witchcraft, and alchemy. This heritage is embedded in urban environments and reminds us that wildness does not have to entail a retreat from the city.

Finally, we can also look to raves and parties as a response to the politically-engaged wildness imagined by Soft Agency.

À la sauvette's film[10] Dance is Politics frames dancing in public space as a temporary suspension of norms and rules from which new political conditions can emerge. They ask what would happen if, instead of smooth paths and bright lights, they designed dancefloors and disco balls. Staging – as proposed by the interventions discussed by à la sauvette throughout this publication – is a provocation and an invitation for festive mobilities of both human and non-human species, to erupt into the public and the counter-public.

John Bingham-Hall

and C. Di Feliciantonio (eds.), *The New Urban Ruins: Vacancy, Urban Politics and International Experiments in the Post-Crisis City*, pp. 53–72.

10 à la sauvette (2021), "Dance is Politics", *Future Architecture Rooms* [futurearchitecturerooms.org/dance-is-politics]

Decolonise the dancefloor
[Habibitch]

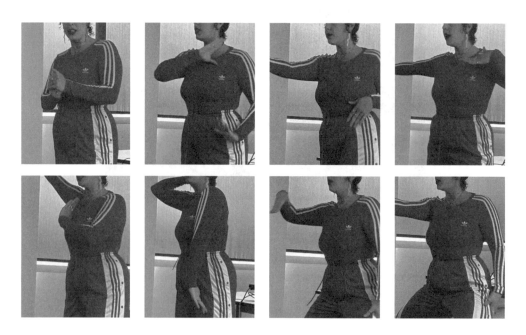

The dancefloor, a safe space?
    A space of liberation, emancipation
    A collective space, a community space, a free space?
Wishes, not realities
There is no such thing as a safe space
    Spaces are structured.
    Spaces are social.
Society is based upon structures of domination.
There is no such thing as a safe space.
    Structures of domination are omnipresent.
    Structures of domination are transversal.
There is no such thing as a safe space.
There is no way out.
No, outside of society.

The dancefloor is a social space and time, where structures
of domination operate.

Everywhere, all the time, on everybody.
Omnipresently and transversally.
What are these domination systems?
    Class – social classes, rich and poor.
    Sex – social sexes, men and women.
    Gender – social genders, cis and trans.
    Race – social races, white and of colour.
Class, sex, gender, race – and more – do not operate in parallels.
I am not; one day I am perceived as a woman,
one day a dyke, one day not rich, one day Algerian.
I am all of those things
Together
All together.
Identities that cross paths.
And this crossroad has a name:
Intersectionality.

The Black Feminism movement has its foundations in the 1960s.
Kimberlé Crenshaw coined the term in 1989. Let's hear her words:
'The complex, cumulative way in which the effects of multiple forms of
discrimination (such as racism, sexism and classism) combine, overlap or
intersect, especially in the experiences of marginalized individuals or groups'.[1]
Everything is said
And the consequence on individuals is:
    Positioning yourself.

1   Crenshaw, K. (1989) "Demarginalizing the Intersection of Race and Sex: A Black Feminist Critique
    of Antidiscrimination Doctrine, Feminist Theory and Antiracist Politics". *University of Chicago*
    Legal Forum, 1(8).

Positioning yourself in society according to the oppressions you experience and/or the privileges you benefit from.
Because if there is oppression, there is privilege.

So let's talk about race, baby.

Let's talk about you and me.

Let's talk about all the good things and the bad things that maybe white people will understand someday.
Without putting ego in the way. (ego kills, no shade)
Because we're talking about structures and not individuals.
Even if there is individual responsibility.
But racism is a system.

Racism is not situational but structural.

Racism is not (only/anymore) a violent, micro-individual hate from extreme-right people.

Racism is systemic and structural, built by centuries of slavery and post-slavery colonisation that left deep marks and created collective imaginaries, vocabularies and behaviours polluted by (white) imperialism.

Because if there is oppression, there is privilege.
And if there are people of colour talking about their oppression, there are white people benefitting from it. (who also should be talking about it – shift the gaze!)
Colonisation is what nowadays society is built upon, sanctifying the white body and the 'white life' as a norm; use of the construction of the subaltern to assert that domination: non-white people, or rather, people of colour.
And white people are benefiting from this system.
Whiteness as a social race, where white people benefit from concrete privileges.
But (and that's an important one)
Where there is oppression, there is always resistance.

And the dancefloor has always been a resistance space.

An ancestral one.

An anti-colonial one.

A flamboyant one.

And what better example than the ballroom scene:

Resistance, resilience, flamboyance.

Back to the late 1960s in the States.
Moment of great political awakening.

Black civil rights movement.

Women's Liberation movement.

Black Feminism.

Anti-war movements.

Hip-hop.

Hip-hop as class resistance.

Hip-hop as race resistance.

The History we know is straight history.

What about gay history?

Queer history?

We have always been here.

But we have to tell our history.

Our queerstory, which is the ballroom.

The ballroom scene was created in that exact same moment of that political awakening. Drag queen competitions were always won by white queens. Black and latinx queens decided to create their own space. For them, by them.

They rented ballrooms in Harlem. They had balls. The community quickly adopted the name of the space they were celebrated in. The ballroom scene was born.

Voguing was not, though.

The performance categories appeared after the fashion, beauty, and realness categories.

All of these being political in themselves. The goal was to incarnate and perform social categories that you were not in real life. That is to say:

> White social categories.
> Rich social categories.
> Straight social categories.
> Cis social categories.
> Rich white cis straight social categories.

To perform them was saying 'I could be that, if society would let me.'

> A statement.
> A political statement.
> An intrinsic political statement.
> An intrinsic political scene.
> The ballroom scene.

Voguing was just all of that being put in movement.

Performing masculinity with the Pop Dip and Spin category, now Oldway.

Performing femininity with the Vogue Femme category, invented by trans women, fem queens in ballroom lingo. All of that within the authority of the Houses and the Parents of the Houses.

Chosen families for the ones rejected.

Gay families for the ones without one.

Queer families with hierarchy, joys, conflicts, shade, empowerment.

A whole recreation of a society where LGBTQ folks of colour are not only accepted but are valorised, celebrated.

Deciding for themselves, representing themselves.

Resisting oppressive norms, racial norms, sex norms, gender norms, class norms.

> All of that in movement.
> All of that with an unequalled flamboyance.

The definition of resilience itself.

So, of course, it had to be lurked upon.

Because everything that shines, white capitalism seizes it.

Everything that shines – as in resists, screams, moves against it – capitalism seizes it. And this has a name:

Cultural appropriation.

A definition:

> Appropriating a culture that is not yours and benefiting from it, capitalistically

and/or symbolically, disrespecting the essence of it with a lack of understanding and acknowledgment of its roots, meanings and values consequently dispossessing key individuals of it.

In other words: 'everything but the burden'.[2]

A decolonial frame:

Cultural appropriation is a colonial continuum because when you can't colonise territories, you colonise cultures. (read that again)

Cultural appropriation is violent and real.

It's colonial violence.

Hence the need to decolonise.

Decolonise our gaze, our thoughts, our practices.

Firstly, decolonising by developing awareness.

Identifying existing domination systems and positioning yourself in these systems:

    Admit what privileges you benefit from, and from there,
    deconstruct yourself and act consequently.
    Don't appropriate codes that are not yours, but also accept to
    make mistakes and be called out without tears.

Secondly, decolonising by deconstructing.

Decolonising History, deconstructing the idea that history is neutral:

    Acknowledge the consequences of colonisation and compel
    ourselves to our collective duty of remembrance.
    Dismantle post-colonial exotism and be vocal about the
    symbolic violence of these colonial clichés.
    Decentre our focus from the Western world to unbuild our vision
    of what is 'universal'.

Thirdly, decolonising by empowering.

Making the invisible visible:

    Allow alternative narratives to emerge and rise.
    Enhance so-called minority cultures while respecting their
    meaning and value to their key individuals.
    Own your identity as a person of colour, speak up, reclaim
    your history and narratives, develop autonomous thinking and
    creative spaces.

To put it simply:

    Listen to key individuals and stop questioning their experiences,
    in order to build allyship and finally decolonise not only the
    dancefloor, but also our entire lives.

2   Tate, G. (ed.) 2003 *Everything but the burden:*
    What white people are taking from black culture.

Wild reading
[Diego Jenowein]

On Saturday, we reconvened for the Mobile Parasitic Reading Room. The rain had kept us inside the day before, but we finally managed to leave the Opale building to try out the exercise in the great outdoors. We all walked to the Parc des Beaumonts, and sat down in a circle once we had reached the top of the small hill in the middle of the park.

We were all given a booklet with a collection of selected texts on wildness. We proceeded to read aloud these different fragments, in no particular order. My booklet was missing a couple of pages – an intentional mistake no doubt, as I had to take my eyes off the print out, only following the voice of the readers with no visual transcription.

The texts in the booklet came to life through these different voices. Reading is generally a tame affair, performed individually by our internal voice, and requires relative silence and absence of disturbances to achieve optimal concentration. Giving voices to these texts in the open, as a collective, gave a different texture to it – like an attempt at rewilding the act of reading.

As I was listening to the successive readings, other sounds joined the group – the leaves shaking in the wind, the children playing in the distance, and snatches of conversations from passers-by, which for a brief moment became parasites of our own parasitic reading room. We kept on reading a few passages as we started walking back to the Opale building. But gradually, the words in the booklet became intertwined with other conversations. Our voices eventually faded out altogether, saturated by surrounding sounds. And the parasitic reading room had dissolved in the city, becoming indistinguishable from the continuous activity of the streets.

Dancing encounters
[Luc Sanciaume]

The morning drizzle turns to heavy rainfall above Montreuil. We are in a steaming meeting space, our bodies dripping in sweat. Ballroom artist Habibitch takes us through the elements of waacking,[1] a dance originating from the black and latinx communities in the 1970s gay clubs of the Californian coast. The atmosphere is ecstatic and as we wander in the space to the beats of disco, soul and funk, our arms roll out vigorously in all directions. This encounter brings me back to my own dance practices of Contact Improvisation (CI) and 5Rhythms (5R),[2] and experiences of embodiment, care, and empowerment. CI and 5R emerged from different milieux to waacking, but both also crystallised in the 1970s, on the north American west coast, amidst the counter cultural movements at the time. There is an implicit correlation between CI and 5R which is to deconstruct binary assumptions in order to imagine more complex interconnected relations between the body, the mind, and the environments in which we move. Improvisation is an important characteristic to both of these dances: in this instance, moving isn't about creating choreographed and alluring gestures, but more about following the immediacy of physical impulses. By focusing on corporeal sensations and subjective feelings, one dives into a form of introspection that is often experienced as therapeutic by unveiling traumas and contributing to self-care.[3] Whilst the subjective experience of dancing is important, there is also much emphasis on the democratisation of the dance floor; by blurring the lines between performer and spectator and queering gender roles and gender expressions. If we consider dance as a cultural construct porous to the ideas transforming society, then these two forms were certainly influenced by the sexual, feminist, and gay liberation movements of the 1960s.[4] Altogether, dance in its spontaneity is a form of wildness: it invites unbridled expressions and less normative behaviours, reminding us that we, as humans, are part of a continuum in which we can find our own agency and our ability to care for ourselves and others.

1   Watch *Warm Up Session with Habibitch* (2021) Film produced by Lafayette Anticipations [lafayetteanticipatios.com/en/manifestation/warm-session-habibitch]

2   Contact Improvisation (CI) originated in 1972 through a series of performances led by Steve Paxton. 5Rhythms (5R) is an ecstatic dance form created by the urban shaman Gabrielle Roth in the mid 1960s.

3   Novack, C.J. (1990) *Sharing the dance: Contact Improvisation and American Culture*, p. 52.

4   Ibid., p. 54.

There is wild in all of us
[Barbara Araque Palacios]

It was a symbiotic encounter, aligned with my own wildness. An opportunity to experience the implications of my identity, when encountering other wild and queer selves. All of us present, acknowledging each others' presence, opening up to find the wild in our own roots, engaging collectively in the act of listening in a safe environment. Discovering a space where I felt free to trace my own embodied practice of resilience, developed at the intersection of my scholarship, architecture, and dance.

Hearing the queer artist-activist Habibitch, and following their workshop on waacking, helped me reconnect with my own process of decolonisation. Dancing has been one of the most empowering and liberating practices of those who have been considered savages: bodies in ecstatic movement, escaping the control of colonial societal constructs, owning the power of the present, and releasing bodily emotions; the very reason why it has been forbidden throughout history. Dance can be a tool for resilience, just like ecological artist David Haley writes:

> 'Create and destroy
> The rhythm of Shiva's drum
> Never stop dancing'[1]

Wildly in nature lies the trance of a body that survives.

Everyone was offered space to engage with their own wildness. Feeling empowered to express not only the appearance of my own barbaric identity, as one of those considered savage, but also to share my ideas formed by my life experience. Feeling understood and being encouraged to be myself helped me to reconnect with my roots, who I am and where I come from. In the end, I discovered, through dance and exchange, each person's sensitive wild experience.

I realised there is wildness in everyone, accepted to a higher or lesser degree. There have been years of efforts to separate human culture from its nature, in what to me appears as a display of fear of that liberating power. But the present demands us to get in touch with that universal root that is nature, including all of those considered wild. It can be retraced in everyone: connecting mind and body, letting our fears out, integrating a new safe space into the wild.

---

1   Haley, D. (2016) "Ecology and the Art of Sustainable Living". *Field Journal*, 4(1): 18.

Movement III

Lisbon

Topographies of Body and Landscape

Climbing the hill and coming down the other side of the hill. Entering the foyer of the palace, an extension of the urban sidewalk. More stairs leading up to other stairs and the courtyard. Up, and down, and off outside we go. Leaves rustle in the sunny courtyard, paved by the same small pieces of limestones the city's pavements are made of. Silver curtains, black rubber floors, and a pink path that leads to the trees become the stage. Twenty strangers become aware of each other as they stand closer. A woman speaks about the purpose of their gathered bodies. In the next days the space will remain the same, but the relation of their bodies will change.

Breathing exercises activate their bodies at first, tuning down together. They gain focus in a field of experimentation by forming crowds, saying words out loud, creating signs, following lines with their bodies, on their bodies, on the ground. Their bodies transfer words from different languages. A sea of words. A sea of moving bodies fills up the pink path, the stone staircase, the dancefloor under the trees. Their moves create new forms and a new space, an intimate space made out of domesticated bodies.

The next day, some of the same bodies meet again. They breathe and laugh and walk together. A wooden floor looks like a giant bed. Bodies lie down and negotiate the distances between them. They stand up to touch the floor, the wall, the door, the railing, the staircase, the rocks, the leaves, the pink path. They move prompted by memories from another time and place. They repeat gestures, and repeat, and repeat until they learn. Until their body memorises. Then they go out to the city.

Eyes on them, on their bodies. They are all dressed in black. They move differently and dance with the metal rusty railings of the park, the curb of the pavement, the door frame, the bollards and the white stones. Their movements create a new vocabulary of urban togetherness.

Back to the courtyard, they need to find a way to fit in their new language, to squeeze in their new memories. How have they forgotten to be together in a smaller space? They remember some of the gestures. Along the way they have created new. The space is no longer the same. Their memories too.

The third and final experimental laboratory of Movement Forum took place in the Sinel de Cordes Palace in Lisbon, and offered us the chance to bring together the two key terms discussed in the previous workshops: the bodies and the cities. On the one hand, the London Lab looked at the sexed and gendered body 'as the locus and site of inscription for specific modes of subjectivity',[1] regulated by social and cultural constructs and forms of representational power. On the other hand, the Paris Lab put the body into the context of urban periphery and the 'wilds', exploring the actual or projected ordering and organisation of its social, cultural, geographical, and ecological relations. The common denominator of the two labs was the ability of the body to be present, move, stay still, expand, cruise, dance, resist, and define its own coordinates in an environment that appears to increasingly deny its rights.

A continuous topography

As an extension of these two labs, the Lisbon Lab then focused on the relationship between bodies and cities as a continuous topography that starts from the interior of the body – a biological, physical and cultural entity – and gradually merges into an environment of architectural objects, physical laws, social negotiations, and legal flows. To suggest such a view of the body-city relationship means to re-examine and question the relationship between biology (body) and culture (city), exploring the way in which culture (re)imagines and (re)produces the body and the ways, in turn, bodies are transformed and 'citified' in an effort to reinscribe and project themselves onto their socio-cultural environment.[2]

The body, as a vehicle that simulates and traverses the city, is 'a concrete, material, animate organization of flesh, organs, nerves, muscles, and skeletal structure which are given a unity, cohesiveness, and organization only through their psychical and social inscription';[3] just like the city. This view of the body puts the focus on its corporeal orientation and exertion; the ways it becomes an extension and reflection of the kind of city it lives into and the kind of landscape it negotiates day by day. The geometries and materiality of a city shape the muscular structure of the body. Its nutritional context affects the well-being of its residents. Infrastructures like streets, pavements, stairs, ramps, elevators, or transport hubs, manage the way bodies move and relate to each other. They control the 'slowness alongside acceleration, blockages, stoppage, and friction as much as liquidity and circulation, and coerced movement as much as freedom of movement'.[4] As philosopher and feminist theorist Elizabeth Grosz argues, 'different cities, different sociocultural environments actively produce the bodies of their inhabitants as particular and distinctive types of bodies, as bodies with particular physiologies, affective lives, and concrete behaviors'.[5]

Uneven environments and mobilities

Lisbon is characterised by an uneven and seemingly inaccessible urban landscape. It is a city defined by steep topography, and an array of steep paths and paved stairs that act as infrastructures to navigate that topography. Although the geometries and materiality of the city do create spaces

1   Grosz, E. (1992) "Bodies – Cities" in B. Colomina (ed.), *Sexuality and Space*, pp. 241-253, p. 241.

2   Ibid., p. 242.

3   Ibid., p. 244.

4   Sheller, M. (2018) *Mobility Justice: The Politics of Movement in an Age of Extremes*, p. 3.

5   Grosz (1992), p. 250.

of humanness, this humanness is also fundamentally limited to assumptions of physical abilities by only able bodies. If 'there is no natural or ideal environment for the body, no "perfect" city, judged in terms of the body's health and well-being',[6] how can that scale of humanness be expanded and celebrated, without excluding non-average forms of mobility?

The inhabitants of Lisbon (Lisboetas) have throughout the years developed mechanisms to navigate its inaccessible and uneven landscape. Supported by trams, buses, electrical bicycles, scooters, or cars, young, adult, and abled bodies have managed to overcome the topography obstacles and interchange between modes of transport. They have expanded the limitations of their own physicality and the limits of the city. And their mobilities have affected the ways the city is experienced and viewed. But what about the bodies that don't fit into the young, adult, non-disabled body category? What about those who have never lived, experienced, or socially trained in such topography? How can the city be reclaimed by a more diverse set of bodies?

Choreographic objects

The workshop took place at the courtyard of the palatian building, a slightly sloping rectangular configuration of a thousand square metres with *calçada portuguesa* (traditional white Portuguese pavement consisting of small pieces of stones), four black rubber surfaces in rectangular and circular shapes that belonged to former playgrounds, two large centennial trees, a stone staircase, several cast-iron benches, and steps. The staging intervention by à la sauvette laid out a long, bright pink piece of fabric from the tree trunks, and the silver curtain hidden inside them, all the way to the

wall of the stone staircase. Emerging from the 'wilds' and whilst making a reference to the theme and set-up of the Paris Lab, the pink path sought to redirect and insert the bodies into the city, 'erasing' the stepped and inaccessible topography that affects their mobility and increases social inequalities between them. The staging also created the spatial conditions of a stage within the courtyard, which allowed all participants to step into a mode of performance and expand their capacities.

That space-stage was then activated for two days by the activities that choreographer Rafael Alvarez, and the architectural theorist Takako Hasegawa led. They both used aural, sometimes visual, prompts to help our bodies instigate new, symbolic and performed, actions, create embodied memories, vocabularies, and choreographic objects, move them into the space or create a new space through them, and register our relationship to time and space by moving, touching, and feeling. Specifically, Alvarez invited us to perform a collection of movement strategies that map our bodies in space in relation to other bodies, the earth, the built and imaginary environment. To build on those experiences, Hasegawa then took us on a journey of translating urban materiality and memories – physical touches, felt senses and meanings – into a series of movements that culminated in a collective gestural vocabulary, which was later re-enacted in the city streets and back at the courtyard of the palace.

Introjections and projections

Moving from the private courtyard to the public street (and back) affected the way we experienced our bodies and how we related to objects and people around us. It felt 'awkward' – quoting Alvarez – because our bodies changed from being private and intimate to being somehow public and public space turned into a private, theatrical

6 Ibid., p. 249.

stage where passers-by and customers from nearby cafes took on the role of the audience. A couple of participants noted that the presence of the camera filming our bodies helped legitimise our own presence and movement outdoors. Others agreed that the black outfits helped too because it seemed like 'we were *making* something instead of just *doing*'.

The kind of awkwardness we felt resulted from the introjections and projections in the relation between the body and its environment, in which both produce each other as 'modes of simulation' based on the image they may have of the other.[7] In other words, while our bodies *simply* moved in the courtyard of the palace, the same movements became a *performance* in the city. Alvarez remarked that, 'there's always a very fine line between being in space and performing, because bodies are always representing something and their identity is always shifting according to the way they decide to present themselves. So, there's always a performative aspect in human movement.'

Performing ideas and memories

According to choreographer William Forsythe, moving is a choreographic object, 'a model of potential transition from one state to another in any space imaginable [... and it...] is by nature open to a full palette of phenomenological instigations because it acknowledges the body as wholly designed to persistently read every signal from its environment.[8] Choreographic thinking assumes the environment – or city – to be a site of potential instigation and organisation of bodily actions and sees any movement within it as a translation of sensorially perceived ideas, emotions, and memories evoked by that site. In that sense, movement differs from dancing because there is a context and cultural meanings associated with it. So, what makes people move in a city and how much does the body avail itself of its surroundings? Which movements are prompted from the environment and which ones belong to the space of memory, desire, fiction, culture, and projection?

While in time we learn to move and repeat a sequence of actions that help the body inhabit and navigate its architectural surroundings, our movements are clearly shaped by the cultural references the body carries. To perform movement is to build on the relation between the two. As Bingham-Hall stressed during the workshop's discussion, his body shifted from an inward focus to an outward one, allowing him to piece together moves inspired by the environment with references from gay men's body language whilst patching symbols onto his body that could communicate things in a heightened or 'camp' way.[9]

The degree to which we can perform our ideas and memories depends on the environment we are to perform them. At the final discussion, people gave examples of cities they had lived in and how these had affected their movement. In Tehran, the body is in flux, constantly finding its way between the cars, avoiding buses passing and people shouting. In Stockholm, people are mindful of where they step, as it is often icy, and keep distances to respect the personal space of others. In London, there are many signs and warnings of do's and don'ts that seek to fully dictate the body, while in Tokyo, everyone is so organised,

7   Ibid., p. 242.

8   Forsythe, W. (2011) "Choreographic objects" in S. Spier (ed.), *William Forsythe and the Practice of Choreography*, pp. 90-92.

9   The first English definition of the term, which appeared in a 1909 edition of the Oxford English Dictionary, was used in a kind of derogatory way to talk about the body language of male homosexuals: "ostentatious, exaggerated, affected, theatrical; effeminate"

obliged, and uniform, that this order gives the body the freedom and time-space to just enjoy the city.

In addition to physical and legal aspects of the city, our performance and movements also depend on the presence of other bodies in that same space. For example, when a female body walks the streets at night alone, carrying feelings of fear, her entire body 'performs' in a way that aims to protect her from harmful interactions. When there is a lack of personal memories, people tend to conform to the behaviour of the majority. Such is the case of visitors who adopt the comportment of locals as a way to align their body to the new cultural context and embody the cultural norms of an environment they are not familiar with in order to grant some kind of permission to be present, occupy space, and move.

The distinction between moving alone and moving with others collectively raises questions about who gets to move where and how performative public spaces can truly be. In a way, it targets the subjectivity of the human body, and how that lies at the core of city making, as a point of reference and form of organisation. Whose subjectivity can inform the way cities are designed? How can we deal with the exclusion created from the point of view of the individual body? How can others feel what we feel? And is there a way to share and exchange our body-memories? Given that certain bodies are absent or excluded from a space, can our bodies act as stand-ins, substitute bodies for others? And if we were to consider a proposal to stand-in, what would that do to the bodies who are not able to perform the action that was meant to be performed by all, and 'what happens to their physicality, their communicative abilities, their voices, and the activity of each fulfilling their presence in the here and now'?[10]

Temporary commons

What we achieved with the explorations of movement in the Lisbon Lab was to gradually shift from a state of publicness with the privilege of anonymity to a state of privacy with the expectations of collectivity. We aligned our bodies with each other, commoned our bodies to build a common ground, and created a form of *temporary commons,* as Rebecca Faulkner pointed out in the group discussion. We rebuilt the relationship of our bodies with the urban space through intimacy, and that intimacy became an infrastructure for the kind of sharing that happens in temporary commons. We all had to actively create it, protect it, and maintain it, because a failure to do so would disrupt the safety and familiarity that was cultivated between us, our bodies, and the city. Together we understood bodily knowledge, memory, and vocabulary as something we don't simply have, but something we *acquire by doing*, whether consciously or unconsciously. So, when choreographers and dancers are given the chance to work with the design of urban spaces, this engagement in doing, embodying, and commoning will be the key.

Fani Kostourou

10 Issa, L. (2009) "When We Are Not: Rehearsing Absence/Presence of a Cultural Body" in A. Bangma, D.M. Donoghue, L. Issa, and K. Zdjelar (eds.),

Something
[Rafael Alvarez]

A collection of bodyscapes, based on personal movement
vocabulary, draws connections between body-space-
presence-travel. A collection of disruptive, abstract, poetic,
and symbolic movements and gestures generate a new
space order, in which we are moving nowhere, together
apart. We choreograph invisible lines that connect us and
simultaneously drive us apart. Through scores and loose
images and ideas, we activate movement and space, and
explore strategies to map the body in urban space.

> Somebody, something, somewhere.
> Anybody, somebody, nobody.
> Somewhere, everywhere, elsewhere.
> From here to there, under where.
> Somewhere there is a place (for us).
> Every body. I have a body, I can move.
> I move, therefore I am.
> I wanna dance with somebody.
> Everybody's looking for something.
> Everybody get up and do your thing.
> City space, body space, no space,
> out of space.

Transit of things　Collect objects and bodies in the city
that generate invisible movement paths and constellations.
Move the city, whilst being moved by it. Imagine your body
as an object, imagine yourself inside that object, install your
object-body in space and travel with it.

From a distance　Find the same distance from two bodies
that keep moving. Adjust constantly your placement
– displacement. Each of your movements alters the
configuration and spatiality of the other bodies in motion,
constantly reorganising the space and its relationship with
others. Each of your actions, gestures, and decisions create
a collective ongoing choreography. The world moves and we
are moved by it.

Small crowds　Stand still in the crowd, feel lost in the crowd,
feel lonely and invisible. Be the crowd and single. Keep a
distance. Find distance from things, growing apart, feeling
apart or departed.

Invisible awareness   Be invisible together. Be present, not moving on the spot, out of space, outer space. Be squeezed in one space. Find yourself in a non-place. Melting camouflaged bodies. Erase your presence in space. Start moving with this 'invisible' awareness. Fade away, let yourself be a faded landscape.

Empty body   Imagine your body as an empty container. Refill your body with water. Move around with your liquid body. Let yourself be submerged by this underwater world. Liquify yourself. Liquid bodies in liquid cities.

Breathing rocks   Walk on the rocks and walk with the rocks, letting yourself be guided by the rocks, moving the rocks. Be a rock. Stand still like a rock. Breathing rocks. You rock my world. Establish contact through the rocks and find ways to establish movement dialogues guided by the rocks.

Impossible images (for impossible bodies)   Climb the stairs to nowhere, a stairway to where. Stare. Try going up with the sensation and awareness of going down. Now reverse the experience and start again. Ask yourself: do you know where you are going? Find yourself and then lose yourself in space.

> 'You're walking.
> And you don't always realize it, but you're always falling.
> With each step you fall forward slightly.
> And then catch yourself from falling.
> Over and over, you're falling.
> And then catching yourself from falling.
> And this is how you can be walking and falling at the same time'.[1]

1 Anderson, L. (1982) "Walking and Falling" [youtube.com/watch?v=GHFCdviF6zU]

Textures of gestures / Movement glossary
[Takako Hasegawa]

It was an invitation.
An invitation to open up a new perspective by moving,
to relate anew to the space, the city, and its architecture.
And perhaps to question what makes us move, while making
conversations with the space and to start asking new
questions about the making of the city and urban environment.

Every day, we register our relationships to space and time by
moving, by touching and navigating with our eyes, senses, and
intentions, with our bodies that constantly shift.
Our ever-changing experiences and spatial perceptions
construct our relational understanding of the environment
and how we exist in the world.

Moving is a different form of learning by doing.
Moving is in fact a constant decision-making,
a study in the act of doing.
Our analogue body is full of imagination and intelligence that
embodies empirical knowledge.
And our body is malleable with so much capacity to unlearn,
learn again, and grow.

Overture

On a sunny day in October 2021, the movement workshop
explored, excavated and expressed embodied ideas of the
interior spaces of the Palacio as well as the urban topography
of the city of Lisbon.

The choreographic explorations turned the participants'
bodies into a medium. A medium to touch, feel, sense,
respond, engage, play, occupy, inhabit, think and reimagine
the space and its construct.
The new embodied interpretations were expressed through
the physicality of the bodies that communicated a reframed
understanding of the city beyond conventions and habits.
The lived experience brought changes to each participant
as to the way of seeing, interpreting, and relating to the
world around.

Here is how the movement workshop went.

Prelude

It was essential for the body and mind to get attuned to
the idea of moving, to be able to respond intuitively and
spontaneously, and to go on an unknown journey together as
a newly formed group.
Collective deep breathing, lying down on the wooden floor
pulled by the gravity, and laughing out loud together with
no reason.
Walking with various intentions in the Palacio's interior
space, negotiating accumulated pace and the complexity of
encountering others.

By then the group became a united body with separate parts
– the power of moving together.

First score

The participants were ready for making conversations
with the space of Palacio and its classical domestic order.
If we move according to the qualities of spaces and places,
what choreography would emerge?
Touching and exploring.
The doors, dusty wooden floors, walls, windows, and curtains.
Textures, material temperatures, height, levels, quality of
light, smell, and sound.
How did the body respond, play, and perhaps find a new way
to engage?
What feelings and senses were conjured up together with
new frames of mind?
The window was no longer just a window, the floor
supported the body differently.
The intended functions were reinterpreted by inquisitive
hands, arms, and bodies.
Then, by repeating the actions, the movements got
registered as physical memories of the body, as a series of
short movement sequences created by each participant.

Second score

And onto the open courtyard, down the stone staircases,
cast iron railings, and then trees.
There, various words and phrases invited the participants
to respond by translating the meaning and felt senses of the
terms into movements.

'corners',
'soft floor',
'tall columns',
'small scale',
'far away views',
'chilly wind through the windows'...

What emerged was a movement glossary, expressing
qualities and intentions in relation to the place, time, and
ideas manifested in the present moment and space.
By repeating these choreographed acts over and over, they
became participants' movement memories and vocabularies.

Third score

Out through the Palacio's gate into the streets of Lisbon
and public spaces.
The idea was to re-enact the movement vocabularies in
the new context by engaging with urban constructs and
found objects.
The attempts to reappropriate movement memories over to
the new reading of the city and its scale were inevitably met
with differences and difficulties.
By interacting with these new relationships, each participant
adopted the movements into new sequences, while further
acting on inquiries with street furniture, coincidences, and
urban behaviours, all playing their roles for the rephrasing
of choreography. New relationships, negotiations, and
adaptations between space and the body in motion.
An invitation to imagine and reflect what might these
experiences suggest in the context of a wider consideration
of mobility in the city, especially in relation to Lisbon's steep
topography.
Peculiar body movements stirred up the sense of space for
the passers-by. Spontaneous performances strayed people's
attention momentarily away. Some changes in atmosphere
were sensed.
Urban choreography in an unexpected context created
alternative notions of relating, new imaginaries of what can
happen next, what can happen if.

Fourth score

Back in the Palacio's courtyard.
Participants re-enacted the movement vocabularies once
again and reconfigured the layers of physical memories that
each one of them had built.
Everyone joined to perform their investigations together and
share the moment.
Various spatial perceptions manifested in each bodily
response.
The resulting collective movement eloquently communicated
personal encounters, embodying the curiosity and concerns
of everyone's mind and body.
A woven tapestry of movement as shared experience
of an experimental architectural dialogue.

Epilogue

Dance is an abstract idea manifested through the physicality
of the body. Architecture is the same; the physical existence
embodying abstract thoughts.
Throughout the workshop, participants performed in a
series of spaces, while engaging with and responding to the
particular qualities of Lisbon's cityscapes.
What has emerged was an urban choreography as a
dynamic constellation of participants' moving bodies in
relation to the built elements and structures, streets and
places, and people's activities and rhythms in the everyday
backdrop.
Moving together invited the participants to learn to trust
themselves and each other with a deep sense of sharing –
a poignant aspect of the choreographic inquiry that could
support the collaborative nature of architecture.
Even more urgent in the post-pandemic society where
human connections and empathy need to be sincerely
reconsidered and embraced in meaningful manners
towards the collective planetary future.

The movement inquiry in architecture continues...

(exhale)

A.

B.

A. Traditional Survey: *stone staircase, small tree, metal handrail, balcony overhang, floor tiles.*

B. Experimental Survey: *smooth stone treads covered in thin coat of sandy dust, sharp tickle as the leaves brush against my neck, paint peels off the metal handrail, sun reflects off neighbouring windows, [...].*

Repetitions, realisations, and positionality
[Victoria Noakes]

Dance has been part of my life from a young age and spatial design for the past decade. As a designer, I have found that theoretical essays on dance and architecture often focus on the final choreography without attempting to understand how the dance-making process can enrich architectural practice. The Lisbon Lab provided me with new bases for understanding the relationship between the two disciplines and allowed me to reflect on my own positionality as an architect.

Lesson one After briefly visiting sites and sifting through surveys, designers proceed to shape the urban topographies in which society unfolds. The movement exercises made me realise the extent to which my urban habits are (sub)consciously conditioned by the designer's choices. Whilst repeating the same sequence of choreographed gestures on different sites, I was able to observe how my body's (dis)abilities expanded or shrank according to the micro-details of each site. By complementing traditional surveying methods with more experimental bodily spatial practices, architects can be better equipped to consider subtle realities in the design process.

Lesson two Compared to verbal and visual skills, interpersonal skills are underrated in the architectural profession. In Lisbon, the choreographic activities required participants to interact with each other by exchanging fictional garments, hugging, or avoiding people and encouraged me to embrace fluctuating states of social (dis)comfort and approach others and the world around me with care. Dance can offer valuable lessons on power-dynamics and social empathy to spatial designers who are willing to explore these inner-realisations.

Interpreting choreographic instructions during the workshop enabled me to explore identities, actions, and spaces beyond my usual perspective. I was able to contemplate my experience as a designer and a moving body, and those of others, and understand how dance methodologies can be used as design tools, especially in the phases of research and collaboration. Particularly when considering the ethical duty of architects to reflect on their inherent biases, dance methodologies can certainly help conceptualise and implement positionality.

Dance-writing the city
[Iro Xyda]

From the very first moment I heard about the Lisbon workshop, Theatrum Mundi's research idea and project of Choreographing the City caught my attention. I interpreted it as an effort to dance-write the city, where moving bodies write their own story, bring their own energy or even silence into a space, create or disrupt their own flow, and that of others, and plan their next move, whilst adjusting to the shape and rhythm of the city.

The workshop took place in a beautiful palace. There was a courtyard, with two trees with big roots, a bright pink cloth, some small rocks, silver curtains reflecting with the sun and waving with the wind, rain, uphill, downhill, benches, stairs, leaves, and several moving bodies. All became part of and contributed to the configuration of that space, transforming it into a *stage*. Bodies met with curiosity and explored what the space offered by throwing their feelings out, getting out of their comfort zones, and learning together.

Outside, the city and its structural limitations led the same bodies to a multitude of small choices, redirections, and manipulations, and caused them to navigate, orient, span distance, and imagine themselves and the city anew. A different kind of stage that created new experiences, made the bodies more socially aware, stimulated their imagination and brought them closer together.

Interestingly, the design of the stage, be it the courtyard or the city, can shape the way bodies move, whether that is a highly choreographed movement or simply walking, and as such, choreographers and architects have things in common. Architects (like choreographers) can turn public space into a stage, shaping the movements of the people (or the dancers) with what the space offers and how the space is designed.

Co-performing (in) the city
[Gloria Calderone]

My attention turns to the inside and
I become attentive to my body.
I perceive.
I am present to myself,
and to what
and who stands around me.
I encounter them.

Entering into the courtyard of Palácio Sinel de Cordes feels like having access to the backstage of the city. A scenery out of time has unexpectedly revealed itself to me, like a secret place with its own qualities of sound, air, and light. There is a sense of calmness, slowness, and discretion. Here, behind the city, I feel protected.

The atmosphere allows me – the same time that it requires me – to establish a connection with my body, or rather rediscover my connection with it. I breathe, and begin to scan my bodily reactions to the space around me. I choose to activate all my senses, not only my sight, and this further augments my perception. I become aware of my own presence in space and that's when I encounter myself.

Slowly, I begin to delve into the space around me with gentle attention, curiosity, and openness. My enchanted body starts to recognise hundreds of small details – little things I had not noticed before – and seeks to relate to them in unusual ways through a new vocabulary of gestures. Although at first my body guided my movements, now it is my interaction with the surroundings that leads them. Through these interactions, my body becomes attuned to the environment, and I realise that my gestures are no longer just mine.

I have just created a new gestural memory linked to specific elements of that environment, both natural and architectural, and from now on, I can repeat similar movements in the presence of similar spatial elements. By carrying that memory and knowledge within me, I can transfer them to other places and other people, and in turn, receive theirs that will expand mine once again. I now know that my gestures are not only mine and others' gestures are not only theirs. Our encounters are about constant exchanges, performative reenactments of the environments we have been in, and the bodily languages we have learned and shared. Together we co-perform the city.

Contributors

ADAM MOORE is a transdisciplinary artist who designs and builds performance installations. He applies choreographic and embodied processes for dance making to works in ceramics, film, painting, sculpture, sound, and text. A Trinity Laban Leverhulme Performing Arts Scholar with an MFA in Dance Creative Practice, his work has been supported by Jerwood Arts, Hypha Studios, UP Projects, Jupiter Artland, and Haarlem Artspace among others.

BARBARA ARAQUE is an architect who graduated from the Central University of Venezuela (UCV) in 2019. With a background in dance and performance art and an interest in the use of digital technologies, Barbara leads a master's research at the ENSAPVS about body data, affection, and sensory spaces. As a transdisciplinary artist, they explore the intersection of human diversity and ecology experience.

DIEGO JENOWEIN is a London-based urban researcher with a particular interest in spatial justice. He has previously worked on documenting forced evictions and advocating for housing rights for displaced people at the French-British border. His current research involves community engagement and focuses on preserving and fostering productive and creative activities across London.

ELAHE KARIMNIA is Senior Lecturer at the University of the West of England and Advisor at Theatrum Mundi. She is an urbanist and architect, engaged in research and teaching at the intersection of urban design and critical theory. She is interested in the politics of design and public space. Elahe holds a PhD from KTH and has studied and worked in Tehran, Stockholm, Toronto, and London.

ELOISE MALTBY MALAND is an interdisciplinary artist and researcher whose practice explores relationships between languages, bodies, and spaces. Having graduated from MA Situated Practice at the Bartlett School of Architecture, she is curious about how we understand our spaces, how they shape our interactions and the stories they hold. Among others, she has shared work at Royal Academy, London; School of Environment and Architecture, Mumbai; and Chilean Conexion Festival, Berlin.

ERNESTO IBÁÑEZ GALINDO is an independent researcher and architect, holding a Diploma in Architecture from ULPGC. His practice focuses on the relationship between city, society, and digital realities. He is co-founder of à la sauvette collective with cultural production in Paris, London, Lisbon, and Berlin. Recognised as a Future Architecture Platform Fellow, his work has been awarded by Archdaily, ISArch Awards, ASAcción, and selected for the XIV BEAU among others.

FANI KOSTOUROU is Associate Director at Theatrum Mundi, leading on research, design, creative development, and the organisation's European programme for Future Architecture and LINA platforms. She is an architect and urbanist, researching, curating events, and writing on design, morphology, critical and transdisciplinary spatial theories, housing, and urban cultures. Fani holds a PhD from UCL Bartlett and teaches at the UCA Canterbury School of Architecture and UAL Central Saint Martins.

FEM_ARC is a Berlin-based collective of architects and artists working on projects from an intersectional feminist angle. In formats such as workshops, a podcast series, audio walks, film and multimedia installations, they propagate artistic strategies that question norms and standards and contribute to the creation of non-discriminatory spaces. Two members of fem_arc, Lara Stöhlmacher, architect and ethnologist, and Noumissa Sidibé, architect and performer, joined the Movement Forum London Lab.

GLORIA CALDERONE is an architect and a PhD student of Urban and Regional Planning in the University of Florence. Her research ranges between urban and social sciences and artistic practices, connected to the right of bodies to experience public spaces in the contemporary city. She specifically investigates the possibilities for urban design and performing arts of cooperating, developing projects of spatial re-meaning through creative methodologies.

HABIBITCH is an Algerian-born Paris-based, non-binary, queer, femme, boss, dancer, choreographer and activist. They invest spaces from the Ballroom Scene to feminist and institutional stages to express themselves creatively and politically. They frequently comment on social and political debates related to race, gender, immigration, and marginalised groups in France and beyond. Their performances and analyses are always intersectional as they decolonize the dance-floor everywhere they go.

HÉCTOR SUÁREZ is a multidisciplinary Canary Islands-born architect. His works focus on the interrelationship between society and contemporary culture. Since 2017, he has worked in different architecture offices and practised independently with the à la sauvette collective. Héctor has lectured in Las Palmas's Founding Festivities, been selected a Fellow of the FA Platform, and has exhibited his work in Gran Canaria, Tenerife, London, Paris, Berlin, and Brussels.

IRO XYDA is a dancer and performer with a sense of rhythm, a feeling for music, and a creative ability to express through movement. Her interests and choreographic research are based on the fact that space creates movement. Architectural and intangible elements of space (such as wind, sun, rain) bring imagination and inspiration to her artistic research.

JOHN BINGHAM-HALL is Co-Director of Theatrum Mundi and an independent researcher interested in performances, infrastructures, and technologies of shared life in the city. With a background in music (Goldsmiths) and architectural theory (UCL Bartlett), he works across artistic, spatial and critical humanities to question and participate in the making of the urban public sphere. He is currently Bannister Fletcher Global Fellow at the University of London Institute in Paris.

LEE CAMPBELL is an artist, poet, writer, experimental filmmaker, Senior Lecturer at the University of the Arts London, curator of regular performance poetry night POW! Play on Words in South London, and founder of Homo Humour, the first of its kind project on contemporary queer male film and moving image practices that explores humour and LGBTQ+ storytelling. Recent publications of his poetry include *Queerlings*, *Powders Press*, *Atticus Review*, and *Otherwise*.

LUC SANCIAUME is an architectural designer, whose work spans across various mediums: architecture, art, dance, and research bearing focus on interdisciplinary collaborations. Luc has previously collaborated with architecture practices and cultural organisations including arc en rêve architecture centre in Bordeaux; Phytology, an arts space and nature reserve in London; Theatrum Mundi; and studio Arthur Casas in São Paulo. He currently works as an architect and planning officer in Brussels.

MAHSA ALAMI FARIMAN is a researcher, educator, and architect with over eight years of professional experience, and qualifications in research, teaching, and architecture. She is a Fellow of the Higher Education Academy and has previously taught at Goldsmiths, University of London (as Associate Lecturer) and Coventry University (as Visiting Critic and Guest Lecturer). She has also worked in a number of multidisciplinary architecture and design practices in Iran.

MARCELLO LICITRA is an all-round creative who is passionate about the mutual interaction between architecture, product design, urbanism, and graphic communication. He approaches design and creative thinking as a problem-solving tool, as a way of identifying and forming relationships between ideas and reality, and as a methodology for improving the connections between people and the products/space they use. Through his work, he explores function, encourages interaction, and differentiates narratives.

MARCOS VILLALBA is a Spanish graphic designer and photographer. He graduated from Central Saint Martins in 2008 and spent the following decade working in London. He currently resides in Montevideo, Uruguay, where he runs a design studio working with clients across the fields of art, culture, and education, as well as self-initiated projects focused on architecture and urbanism. He collaborates with Theatrum Mundi in digital projects, publications, and exhibitions.

PABLO CASTILLO LUNA is an architect and master student at Harvard GSD. His socio-political and urban approach in work is rooted at the intersection between critical spatial practice, research, and architectural design. In 2020 he co-founded à la sauvette, an international architecture collective dedicated to design, research, and cultural production. Pablo is currently a researcher at metaLAB (at) Harvard and a Fellow of Real Colegio Complutense and Fundación Mapfre Guanarteme.

RAFAEL ALVAREZ is a choreographer and dancer, set and costume designer, researcher, and teacher. In the last twenty-four years he has investigated the visual dimension of movement and composition. His work stands out for the symbolic, poetic, and minimalist use of body, dance, and space. He explores dance in relation to communities and the inclusive dimension of artistic practices. Rafael is also the founder and artistic director of BODYBUILDERS.

REBECCA FAULKNER is a spatial practitioner, researcher, and writer. Borrowing from varied disciplines, she employs critical writing and performance-based work to explore themes which range from the gendering and governance of public space to the extractive process of mining finite resources. Presently, she practices at Periscope, performs as a member of Musarc, and advocates for mental health awareness through the Architect's Benevolent Society.

SANTIAGO CONFALONIERI is a Uruguayan creative and graphic designer. He is interested in the different actors that influence contemporary society. He's passionate about collaborative and interdisciplinary projects addressing different aspects of art, culture, and education in order to generate different discourses and alternative ways of inhabiting society. He is currently working at Villalba Studio and studying Visual Communication Design at the Universidad de la República in Uruguay.

SARA WOOKEY's transdisciplinary research across architecture, choreography, sociology, and museology is informed by her twenty-eight years as an internationally recognised dance practitioner. Her current concern is how dance and expanded choreography change the human imaginary of relationships between bodies and space in ways that can be more inclusive and sustainable. Affiliates include Tate Modern, Art Science Museum Singapore, Van Abbemuseum, Tavistock Institute, Victoria & Albert Museum, and Coventry University.

TAKAKO HASEGAWA engages with movement as an agency for architectural thinking and its creative process by cross-pollinating contemporary dance with architecture, exploring architectural experience as embodied choreographies. Founder of Dancing Architects, a transdisciplinary research platform, she is currently pursuing her PhD at the Architectural Association School of Architecture in London focusing on architectural pedagogy through choreographic explorations that bring changes towards transformative learning.

VICTORIA NOAKES' work is rooted in the intersection of performance, theory and art, is energetic, eclectic, and often gravitates towards non-conformity. With a background in architecture and dance, Victoria uses the body, and alternative mapping techniques, as tools to understand complex issues and narratives within the built environment. With a particular focus on water, bodies and cities, their inter-disciplinary practice offers new perspectives on how these intersect.

Editorial: Fani Kostourou, Elahe Karimnia
Project Curatorial: Fani Kostourou, John Bingham-Hall, Elahe Karimnia
Design: Marcos Villalba, Santiago Confalonieri
Proofreading: The Book Edit
Typeface: Neue Haas Unica
Printing: Print Love, York

Image captions and credits
Front cover: illustration © Marcello Licitra
p. 8 illustration © à la sauvette
pp. 18, 35 photos © Fani Kostourou
pp. 19, 20 photos © à la sauvette
pp. 21, 36-39, 44, 65, 67-70 photos © Rebecca Faulkner
pp. 23, 26 drawings © various contributors
p. 40 photo © Héctor Suárez
p. 51 illustration © Mahsa Alami Fariman
pp. 60-61, 66, 86-87 photos © John Bingham-Hall
pp. 85, 88-89 photos © Takako Hasegawa
p. 96 illustration © Victoria Noakes

We would like to thank all the contributors for the provision of original texts and illustrations and the partner organisations and individuals who have collaborated with Theatrum Mundi in the work presented in this edition:

Adam Moore, Amandine Canistro, Andrés Avila Reyes, Anna Sofia Lekander, Anna Ulrikke Andersen, Aseem Inam, Bárbara Araque Palacios, Christian Kipp, Diego Jenowein, Dimitri Szuter, Elahe Karimnia, Ellie Cosgrove, Eloise Maltby Maland, Ernesto Ibáñez Galindo, Eunsoo Jang, Fani Kostourou, Gloria Calderone, Habibitch, Helene, Héctor Suárez González, Iro Xyda, Joanna Kuczora, John Bingham-Hall, Joseph Kai, Julia Albani, Lara Stöhlmacher, Laura Davy, Laura Narvaez Zertuche, Lee Campbell, Luc Sanciaume, Mahsa Alami, Marta Michalowska, Marzia Magnanini, Mikaela Psarra, Noumissa Sidibé, Oceane Ragoucy, Pablo Castillo Luna, Phoebe Eddleston, Rafael Alvarez, Rebecca Faulkner, Rosario Talevi, Rui Filipe Antunes, Sara el Samman, Sara Wookey, Sebastien Millot, Stephanie, Takako Hasegawa, Victoria Noakes, Youmna Saba, Lou Marcellin, Labeja Kodua Okullu, Amin Taha, Groupwork, Plateau Urbain, Inely's Cake, Aziza Gonon, Lisbon Architecture Triennale, Manuel Henriques, Isabel Antunes, Sara Battesti, Carolina Vicente, Joana Fernandes, A Cozinha d'Anita, Ana Primavera, Nuno Dionisio, Vitor Hugo Costa, Future Architecture Platform, Matevž Čelik, Milan Dinevski, Tanja Vergles.

This publication is part of Theatrum Mundi Editions, a quarterly series reflecting current streams and new directions in our research, led by our team and collaborators, and shared with our members. Editions are generously supported by the Friends of Theatrum Mundi.

Friends of Theatrum Mundi
(see https://theatrum-mundi.org/become-a-member/)
CSM MA Cities MA Cities, Central Saint Martins

Rudi Christian Ferreira

Catherine Visser

David Chipperfield Architects

João Villas

Theatrum Mundi
c/o Groupwork
15A Clerkenwell Close
EC1R 0AA
London, UK

Theatrum Mundi Europe
59 Rue du Département
75018
Paris, France

www.theatrum-mundi.org

ISBN 978-1-9161864-9-1

The project, Movement Forum, and this publication, Encounters, are part of the Future Architecture platform programme co-funded by the Creative Europe Programme of the European Union. The content of the publication reflects the views of the authors and can in no way be taken to reflect the views of the European Union.

Co-funded by the
Creative Europe Programme
of the European Union